Teens and Alcohol

Other books in the Current Controversies series:

The Abortion Controversy
Alcoholism
Assisted Suicide
Biodiversity
Capital Punishment
Censorship
Child Abuse
Computers and Society
Conserving the Environment
Crime
The Disabled
Drug Legalization
Drug Trafficking
Ethics
Europe
Family Violence
Free Speech
Garbage and Waste
Gay Rights
Genetic Engineering
Guns and Violence
Hate Crimes
Hunger
Illegal Drugs
Illegal Immigration
The Information Highway
Interventionism

Iraq
Marriage and Divorce
Medical Ethics
Mental Health
Minorities
Nationalism and Ethnic
   Conflict
Native American Rights
Police Brutality
Politicians and Ethics
Pollution
Prisons
Racism
Reproductive Technologies
The Rights of Animals
Sexual Harassment
Sexually Transmitted Diseases
Smoking
Suicide
Teen Addiction
Teen Pregnancy and Parenting
Urban Terrorism
Violence Against Women
Violence in the Media
Women in the Military
Youth Violence

Teens and Alcohol

James D. Torr, *Book Editor*

Daniel Leone, *President*
Bonnie Szumski, *Publisher*
Scott Barbour, *Managing Editor*

CURRENT CONTROVERSIES

Cover photo: © Tony Stone Images

Library of Congress Cataloging-in-Publication Data

Teens and alcohol / James D. Torr, book editor
     p. cm. — (Current controversies)
   Includes bibliographical references and index.
   ISBN 0-7377-0859-X (lib. bdg. : alk. paper) — ISBN 0-7377-0858-1 (pbk. : alk. paper)
    1. Teenagers—Alcohol use—United States. 2. Alcoholism—United States—Prevention. I. Torr, James D., 1974– II. Series.

HV5135 .T445   2002
362.292'2'08350973—dc21   2001033686

© 2002 by Greenhaven Press, Inc., 10911 Technology Place, San Diego, CA 92127
Printed in the U.S.A.

Contents

The Problem of Underage Drinking Is Exaggerated

Chapter 2: What Problems Are Associated with Teen Alcohol Abuse?

Chapter 3: Does Alcohol Advertising Encourage Teens to Drink?

Yes: Alcohol Advertisements Promote Underage Drinking and Should Be Restricted

want to preempt their competitors in establishing brand loyalty among young people.

No: Alcohol Advertising Does Not Cause Teens to Drink

one, and continue to fall each year. However, levels of excessive and abusive drinking among young people only began increasing *after* the federal government mandated that states raise their drinking age to twenty-one.

Chapter 5: What Measures Are Effective in Reducing Teen Alcohol Abuse?

    The simplest and most effective way to reduce underage drinking is to
    reduce minors' access to alcohol. High school and college students often
    obtain alcohol through the use of fake, altered, or borrowed ID cards. Pro-
    grams in which law enforcement agents and alcohol beverage retailers are
    trained to spot false IDs can help combat this problem.

Foreword

By definition, controversies are "discussions of questions in which opposing opinions clash" (Webster's Twentieth Century Dictionary Unabridged). Few would deny that controversies are a pervasive part of the human condition and exist on virtually every level of human enterprise. Controversies transpire between individuals and among groups, within nations and between nations. Controversies supply the grist necessary for progress by providing challenges and challengers to the status quo. They also create atmospheres where strife and warfare can flourish. A world without controversies would be a peaceful world; but it also would be, by and large, static and prosaic.

The Series' Purpose

The purpose of the Current Controversies series is to explore many of the social, political, and economic controversies dominating the national and international scenes today. Titles selected for inclusion in the series are highly focused and specific. For example, from the larger category of criminal justice, Current Controversies deals with specific topics such as police brutality, gun control, white collar crime, and others. The debates in Current Controversies also are presented in a useful, timeless fashion. Articles and book excerpts included in each title are selected if they contribute valuable, long-range ideas to the overall debate. And wherever possible, current information is enhanced with historical documents and other relevant materials. Thus, while individual titles are current in focus, every effort is made to ensure that they will not become quickly outdated. Books in the Current Controversies series will remain important resources for librarians, teachers, and students for many years.

In addition to keeping the titles focused and specific, great care is taken in the editorial format of each book in the series. Book introductions and chapter prefaces are offered to provide background material for readers. Chapters are organized around several key questions that are answered with diverse opinions representing all points on the political spectrum. Materials in each chapter include opinions in which authors clearly disagree as well as alternative opinions in which authors may agree on a broader issue but disagree on the possible solutions. In this way, the content of each volume in Current Controversies mirrors the mosaic of opinions encountered in society. Readers will quickly realize that there are many viable answers to these complex issues. By questioning each author's conclusions, students and casual readers can begin to develop the critical thinking skills so important to evaluating opinionated material.

Current Controversies is also ideal for controlled research. Each anthology in the series is composed of primary sources taken from a wide gamut of informational categories including periodicals, newspapers, books, United States and foreign government documents, and the publications of private and public organizations. Readers will find factual support for reports, debates, and research papers covering all areas of important issues. In addition, an annotated table of contents, an index, a book and periodical bibliography, and a list of organizations to contact are included in each book to expedite further research.

Perhaps more than ever before in history, people are confronted with diverse and contradictory information. During the Persian Gulf War, for example, the public was not only treated to minute-to-minute coverage of the war, it was also inundated with critiques of the coverage and countless analyses of the factors motivating U.S. involvement. Being able to sort through the plethora of opinions accompanying today's major issues, and to draw one's own conclusions, can be a complicated and frustrating struggle. It is the editors' hope that Current Controversies will help readers with this struggle.

Greenhaven Press anthologies primarily consist of previously published material taken from a variety of sources, including periodicals, books, scholarly journals, newspapers, government documents, and position papers from private and public organizations. These original sources are often edited for length and to ensure their accessibility for a young adult audience. The anthology editors also change the original titles of these works in order to clearly present the main thesis of each viewpoint and to explicitly indicate the opinion presented in the viewpoint. These alterations are made in consideration of both the reading and comprehension levels of a young adult audience. Every effort is made to ensure that Greenhaven Press accurately reflects the original intent of the authors included in this anthology.

Introduction

"Undoubtedly, alcohol is the principal drug use problem in America today," said drug czar Barry McCaffrey, the director of the Office of National Drug Control Policy (ONDCP), in 1997. Most public health advocates agree. "Alcohol is the drug most frequently used by American teenagers," writes Surgeon General David Satcher. "Parents don't realize that alcohol—not illicit drugs—is the No. 1 drug killing our children," says Karolyn Nunnallee, president of Mothers Against Drunk Driving (MADD). "They think, 'Thank God my child is only drinking beer and not using drugs.' We've got to change that mindset."

The costs of teen alcohol abuse are staggeringly high. According to Satcher, alcohol "is consumed more frequently than all other illicit drugs combined and is the drug most likely to be associated with injury or death. Alcohol is a drug that can affect judgment, coordination and long-term health. It is involved in teen automobile crashes, homicides, and suicides—the three leading causes of teen deaths." The National Highway Traffic Safety Commission reports that over two thousand young people die in alcohol-related crashes each year. According to the National Institute on Alcohol Abuse and Alcoholism (NIAAA), youth who drink before age fifteen are four times more likely to develop alcohol dependence than those who begin drinking at age twenty-one.

According to David Byrd, a writer for the *National Journal*, "Although no one denies the problem of underage drinking, its surprising magnitude has received scant attention." Because of this, many public health advocates believe that reducing underage drinking should be a goal in the war on drugs. "No comprehensive drug control strategy for youth can be complete without the full inclusion of underage alcohol use and abuse," writes the surgeon general. McCaffrey himself has said that alcohol is "the most dominant drug causing violence among young people."

But alcohol is *not* part of ONDCP's drug prevention efforts. In 1999, MADD led a coalition calling on Congress to pass the Roybard-Allard amendment, which would have included alcohol in ONDCP's five-year, $1 billion anti-drug advertising campaign. In July 1999 however, the measure was voted down. "Not one penny of taxpayer dollars will purchase underage drinking prevention ads," laments MADD national director of programs Bobby Heard. In a news conference following the congressional vote, McCaffrey explained that including alcohol in the war on drugs "could dilute the focus . . . and would only hamper the effectiveness of our campaign." "Alcohol is a legal substance, and these other drugs are not legal," said Robert Weiner, a spokesman for McCaffrey.

Weiner's statement echoes the alcohol industry's own arguments against targeting alcohol. Since alcohol is legal for adults, the industry questions whether it is within ONDCP's jurisdiction to campaign against it. Moreover, industry spokesmen object to the idea that alcohol is as harmful as illegal drugs. "A glass of chardonnay with our meals should not be equated with cocaine or heroin," says John DeLuca, president of the Wine Institute, a trade association. "Such a monstrous distortion offends culture, tradition, social science, and common sense." David Rehr, vice president of the National Beer Wholesalers Association argues that "our adversaries want . . . to give people the idea that sipping a beer is like injecting yourself with heroin, which it's not."

Supporters of Roybard-Allard, however, questioned whether the amendment had failed because of the alcohol industry's enormous influence on Capitol Hill. "Alcohol interests are likely to fiercely challenge any taxpayer-funded advertising campaign trying to 'deglamorize' drinking," notes *National Journal*'s David Byrd. Philip Morris, the company that owns Miller Brewing, was the largest donator to the Republican Party in 1998, and Joseph E. Seagram & Sons was the top donor to the Democrats in 1996, giving a total of over $1.2 million. "Illegal drug producers don't provide PAC [political action committee] money," says George Hacker, head of the Alcohol Policies project at the Center for Science in the Public Interest.

To its credit, in 1998 Congress created a new program in the Office of Juvenile Justice and Delinquency Prevention. The Congressional Combating Underage Drinking Initiative provides at least $360,000 to each state to help stop illegal alcohol sales to minors and create new programs to prevent underage drinking. But the program's $25 million budget is minuscule compared to ONDCP's $1 billion initiative or to the $1.4 billion that Anheuser-Busch spent on advertising in 1999 alone. Lobbyists such as Hacker believe that a much greater portion of the nation's resources should be devoted to the problem of underage drinking. "Either [lawmakers] stand up to protect America's children, or they stand up for the alcoholic beverage industry's special interests," he concludes.

The ongoing debate over how the government should deal with the problem of underage drinking is just one of the issues examined in *Teens and Alcohol: Current Controversies*. Other aspects of the problem are explored in the following chapter: How Serious Is the Problem of Underage Drinking? What Problems Are Associated with Teen Alcohol Abuse? Does Alcohol Advertising Encourage Teens to Drink? Are Age-21 Laws Effective in Reducing Teen Alcohol Abuse? What Measures Are Effective in Reducing Teen Alcohol Abuse? The volume aims to raise awareness about the often-ignored issue of underage drinking and to educate readers about the varied approaches to preventing teen alcohol abuse.

Chapter 1

How Serious Is the Problem of Underage Drinking?

Alcohol Use Among Adolescents: An Overview

by Patrick O'Malley, Lloyd D. Johnston, and Jerald G. Bachman

About the authors: *Patrick O'Malley, Lloyd D. Johnston, and Jerald G. Bachman are research scientists at the University of Michigan.*

Many American adolescents use alcohol, even though the minimum legal drinking age is 21. This article describes the extent and nature of alcohol use among American adolescents. In addition, the article provides information on trends in, self-reported reasons for, and consequences of adolescent alcohol use. The article draws on information from the Monitoring the Future (MTF) study, the National Household Survey on Drug Abuse (NHSDA), and the Youth Risk Behavior Survey (YRBS), which are described in the following section. The discussion emphasizes, however, findings from the MTF study.

Prevalence of Alcohol Use Among Adolescents

Several major ongoing national surveillance systems collect and evaluate information on alcohol use patterns among adolescents:.
- The MTF study, which is conducted under a research grant to the University of Michigan from the National Institute on Drug Abuse.
- The NHSDA, which is conducted by the Substance Abuse and Mental Health Services Administration (SAMHSA).
- The YRBS, which is conducted by the Centers for Disease Control and Prevention (CDC).

The MTF study, which uses a school-based sample, has conducted annual surveys of nationally representative samples of high school seniors since 1975 and of 8th and 10th grade students since 1991. It surveys about 50,000 students per year, using self-completed questionnaires administered under confidential conditions in classrooms. The study is designed to provide estimates of alcohol and other drug use and of related attitudes and beliefs among the Nation's secondary school students.

Reprinted from "Alcohol Use Among Adolescents," by Patrick O'Malley, Lloyd D. Johnston, and Jerald G. Bachman, in *Alcohol Health and Research World*, vol. 22, no. 2, 1998.

Teens and Alcohol

The NHSDA surveys a nationally representative, household-based sample of Americans age 12 and older. The surveys are conducted as face-to-face interviews, with self-administered forms used for sensitive questions. In recent years, the surveys have been conducted annually. Youth samples have varied in size; the most recent survey, conducted in 1997, included 7,844 individuals ages 12 to 17. The NHSDA is designed to provide annual estimates of alcohol and other drug use among the Nation's general population.

The school-based YRBS, which has been conducted biennially since 1991, surveys high school students in grades 9 through 12 using self-completed questionnaires administered under confidential conditions in classrooms. Sample sizes have varied; the 1997 survey included 16,262 students. The YRBS is designed to provide estimates of various risk behaviors, including some measures of alcohol and other drug use, among the Nation's high school students.

Although none of the three surveillance systems is devoted entirely, or even primarily, to alcohol-related material, each includes data on alcohol use among American adolescents. The scope of this information, however, is somewhat limited. For example, although all three surveys evaluate patterns of recent alcohol use, information on other aspects of alcohol consumption (e.g., the respondents' family histories of alcohol use and abuse, expectancies about alcohol use, methods of obtaining alcohol, and consequences of alcohol use) is sketchier.

Analyses of the most recent data from the three survey systems found high rates of alcohol use and relatively low rates of complete abstention among American adolescents, as follows:.

- The 1997 MTF study found that 54 percent of 8th graders (almost all of whom are ages 13 to 14) reported having consumed alcohol (i.e., more than just a few sips) in their lifetime. The corresponding rates for 10th graders (i.e., ages 15 to 16) and 12th graders (i.e., ages 17 to 18) were 72 percent and 82 percent, respectively.
- The 1996 NHSDA reported that 39 percent of adolescents ages 12 to 17 had drunk alcohol. The study also noted a sharp age-related increase in alcohol use, with 14 percent of 12- to 13-year-olds, 39 percent of 14- to 15-year-olds, and 62 percent of 17- to 18-year-olds reporting previous alcohol consumption.
- According to the 1997 YRBS, 79 percent of students in grades 9 through 12 had consumed alcohol. In this survey, the rates of alcohol use increased steadily from 72 percent among 9th graders to 84 percent among 12th graders.

Despite the consistent finding that relatively few Americans are complete abstainers by their late teens, substantial differences exist among the surveys with respect to the specific rates of alcohol consumption for the various age groups. Some of the differences may result from the specific design of each survey. For example, some studies include only students who are still in school (e.g., the MTF study), whereas other studies (e.g., the NHSDA) also include school dropouts, who may be at higher risk for alcohol use. Furthermore, the MTF study and the YRBS are school based, whereas the NHSDA is conducted in a home setting where parents may be present, which may lead to greater reluctance to report deviant behavior. Differences among the surveys in the wording of the questions and in the way in which the survey is administered (i.e., interview versus self-administered questionnaire) also may affect the outcome and account for some of the discrepancies in the findings obtained.

Differences Among Demographic Subgroups

The MTF study assesses both the prevalence of alcohol use and the prevalence of getting drunk among 8th, 10th, and 12th graders. To this end, respondents are asked, "Have you ever had any beer, wine, wine coolers, or liquor to drink—more than just a few sips?" Respondents who answer affirmatively then are asked: "On how many occasions have you had alcoholic beverages to drink—more than just a few sips . . . during the last 30 days?" and "On how many occasions (if any) have you been drunk or very high from drinking alcoholic beverages . . . during the last 30 days?" From these data, the prevalence of alcohol use and having been drunk can be determined for the entire sample as well as for various demographic subgroups based on gender, race, region of the country where the students live, population density of the area, parental education, and family structure. Among the most recent (i.e., 1997) results obtained for 12th graders, the following were particularly noteworthy:

> *"The 1997 MTF study found that 54 percent of 8th graders . . . reported having consumed alcohol in their lifetime."*

• The prevalence of alcohol use and of having been drunk were remarkably high. More than one-half of the 12th graders reported having had at least one drink—and more than one-third reported having been drunk at least once—in the past 30 days.

• Male students were more likely than female students to report drinking, although by only a relatively small margin (56 percent versus 49 percent). The gender difference was greater for having been drunk (39 percent versus 29 percent).

• The prevalence of both drinking and being drunk was highest in the Northeast region of the United States, but regional differences were rather small.

• Drinking rates differed only slightly by population density (i.e., metropolitan statistical area). Somewhat greater differences existed in the rates of being drunk, with students in more rural areas (i.e., counties where the largest city has a population less than 50,000) exhibiting the highest rates.

• Higher parental education (which serves as a proxy for higher socioeconomic status) was associated with increased rates of alcohol use and being drunk. Conversely, the association between family structure (operationalized as whether the student reported living with two parents versus one or no parents) and drinking status was weak and inconsistent.

- With respect to the three largest racial/ethnic subgroups, the rates of drinking and being drunk were lowest among African-American 12th graders, highest among white 12th graders, and intermediate among Hispanic 12th graders. Reliable national estimates of alcohol use among other racial/ethnic subgroups (e.g., Asian-Americans or Native Americans) are more difficult to obtain, because their numbers are too low

> *"Male students were more likely than female students to report drinking."*

in national surveys. Bachman and colleagues (1991), using data from the 1976 to 1989 MTF surveys, showed that Asian-American 12th graders had low rates of alcohol use, whereas Native American 12th graders had relatively high rates of use. Similarly, combined data from the 1991 to 1993 NHSDAs have indicated that Asian-American youth ages 12 to 17 have lower rates of alcohol use (as measured by prevalence of use in the past year) than do African-American youth. Even with the combined data, the NHSDA did not include enough Native American youth respondents to characterize that population.

Taken together, the data indicate that adolescent alcohol use has permeated all sociodemographic subgroups of society to a similar extent: In general, only minor differences exist among sociodemographic subgroups defined by geographical region, population density, parental education, and family structure. Those minor variations are less than they were 20 years ago, when differences were substantial, particularly with respect to region and population density.

Developmental Differences

The prevalence of alcohol use and of having been drunk increases sharply during adolescence; rates are substantially higher among 12th graders than among 8th graders. Nevertheless, a considerable proportion of 8th graders already uses alcohol, with one-fourth of the students reporting having had a drink in the past 30 days. Moreover, one in three of those drinkers (i.e., one-twelfth of the total sample) reported having consumed enough alcohol to get drunk or very high.

Developmental differences also existed in the associations of various sociodemographic factors with drinking behavior. For example, in 8th grade, little difference existed between boys and girls in their rates of drinking (25 percent for boys versus 24 percent for girls) or having been drunk (8.4 percent for boys versus 7.9 percent for girls). By 12th grade, however, substantial gender differences in drinking behavior emerged. Similarly, parental education levels, which were positively related to alcohol use among 12th graders, were negatively related to alcohol use among 8th graders: Students with higher parental education were less likely to drink in 8th grade than were students with lower parental education. Among 12th grade students, however, drinking levels were higher among those with higher parental education. This change in the relationship between drinking level and parental education likely results at least in part from the fact that some students drop out of school before 12th grade. Those students are more likely to (a) use alcohol and get drunk and (b) come from homes with lower parental education levels than are students who stay in school. Consequently, if school dropouts were included in the 12th-grade surveys, the association of drinking levels with parental education would be less positive.

Among the three largest racial/ethnic groups evaluated in the MTF study, African-American students reported the lowest rates of drinking and getting drunk at all three grade levels. Hispanic and white students had similar rates in 8th grade, but a difference in the rates of getting drunk emerged by 10th grade, with whites having higher rates. This difference increased further by 12th grade. Analyses reported elsewhere support a "school dropout" effect as the most likely interpretation for the emerging difference. This hypothesis posits that substantially higher dropout rates between 10th and 12th grade among Hispanic youth compared with white youth produce a more biased sample of Hispanic youth by 12th grade, because dropouts are more likely to use alcohol or get drunk.

Differences Based on Behavioral and Attitudinal Variables

The MTF study also analyzed the prevalence of drinking or having been drunk in subgroups of adolescents based on several behavioral and attitudinal variables (i.e., religious commitment, grade-point average GPA , truancy rates, and evenings out per week). Each of those variables was associated rather strongly with the adolescents' drinking behaviors, either in a positive or a negative manner. Moreover, in contrast to the sociodemographic factors, the influences of these variables were similar for all three age groups, although the associations tended to get stronger with increasing age.

The behavioral factor that exhibited the strongest association with drinking behavior was the number of evenings that respondents reported going out for fun and recreation in a typical week. Thus, among 12th graders, 52 percent of those who went out 4 or more evenings a week reported getting drunk during the past 30 days, compared with 30 percent of those who went out 2 evenings a week and 14 percent of those who went out fewer than 2 nights a week. Similar differences already existed among 8th graders, with rates of getting drunk of 15 percent, 7 percent, and 4 percent among those who went out 4 or more nights, 2 nights, or fewer than 2 nights per week, respectively.

> *"African-American students reported the lowest rates of drinking and getting drunk."*

A similar positive association existed between truancy rates and alcohol use: Students with high truancy rates were far more likely than students with low truancy rates to be drinkers or to get drunk. For example, highly truant 12th graders were 2.5 times as likely as 12th graders with low truancy rates to report having been drunk in the past month (57 percent versus 23 percent).

In contrast to the frequency of going out and truancy, the students' religious commitment (as determined by how important religion is to the student and how often he or she attends religious services) and GPA were negatively associated with the prevalence of drinking and being drunk. For example, only 40 percent of 12th graders with a high degree of religious commitment reported having drunk any alcohol in the past 30 days, compared with 60 percent of students with a low religious commitment. A similar relationship existed with respect to GPA: Whereas 45 percent of 12th grade students whose GPA was "A" drank alcohol in the past 30 days, 58 percent of students with a GPA of "B-minus" or lower did so. The association between GPA and drinking behavior was even stronger among 8th grade students, where approximately twice as many of the students with lower GPAs had consumed alcohol compared with those with the highest GPAs.

Association Between Alcohol Use and Use of Other Drugs

One important reason for concern about adolescent alcohol use is its close association with the use of other drugs. There is considerable evidence that alcohol use tends to precede use of illicit drugs, and some researchers have argued, based on longitudinal data, that alcohol use serves as a "gateway" to the use of illicit substances. Analyses of the MTF study data have demonstrated that the cross-sectional association between alcohol and other drug use also is strong. For example, among 8th graders who had not consumed alcohol at any time in their lives, only 3 percent had smoked cigarettes in the past 30 days or used marijuana in the past 12 months, and fewer than 0.5 percent had used cocaine in the past 12 months. Among 8th graders who had consumed alcohol at least 40 times in their lives, in contrast, approximately two-thirds had smoked cigarettes in the past 30 days or used marijuana in the past 12 months, and 18 percent had used cocaine in the past 12 months. Similar associations between alcohol consumption and other drug use existed among both 10th and 12th graders.

Problems Caused by Adolescent Alcohol Use

Another reason for concern about adolescent alcohol use is the risk of serious social, medical, and legal problems that can result from alcohol consumption, such as impaired performance at school or work; interpersonal problems with friends, family members, teachers, and supervisors; physical and psychological impairment; and drunk driving. To assess the prevalence of such problems among alcohol-consuming adolescents, the MTF survey asked 12th graders whether alcohol had ever caused them any of 15 potential problems. Among the students in the 1994 to 1997 surveys who had consumed alcohol on at least 10 occasions during their lifetimes (i.e., 53 percent of all 12th graders surveyed), almost two-thirds (i.e., 62 percent) had experienced one or more of those problems. Specifically, approximately 15 percent of the drinking 12th graders reported one problem, 13 percent reported two problems, and 34 percent reported three or more problems. Thus, a remarkable 18 percent of all 12th graders (i.e., 34 percent of 53 percent who had consumed alcohol on 10 or more occasions) had experienced 3 or more different alcohol-related problems, despite the fact that virtually none of them had reached the minimum legal drinking age. Similar results also were obtained in the NHSDA, which found that 38 percent of respondents ages 12 to 17 who reported drinking some alcohol in the past year had experienced at least one alcohol-related problem.

"Students with high truancy rates were far more likely . . . to be drinkers or to get drunk."

The most common alcohol-related problem, which was reported by approximately one-half of the drinkers, was that alcohol use caused the respondent to behave in ways that he or she later regretted. Furthermore, almost one-third of the drinkers reported that alcohol use had interfered with their ability to think clearly. Another common and potentially serious problem was unsafe driving because of alcohol, which was reported by approximately one in five adolescent drinkers. Similarly common were alcohol-related interpersonal problems with significant others and parents.

Reasons for Adolescent Alcohol Use

The MTF study also explored the reasons why so many young people drink alcohol. When asked for the most important reasons why they drank alcoholic beverages, 12th graders primarily emphasized the pleasurable aspects of drinking. For example, almost three-fourths of all 12th graders who had ever consumed alcohol gave "to have a good time with friends" as one of their reasons. Other commonly cited motivations related to alcohol's pleasurable effects referred to alcohol's good taste, its ability to make you feel good or high, and its ability to relax or relieve tension. Also high on the list of reasons for alcohol consumption was curiosity about alcohol and its effects, which was cited by approximately one-half of the respondents.

In contrast, substantially fewer adolescents reported using alcohol for coping with problematic situations. Thus, approximately one-fourth of 12th graders who ever consumed alcohol indicated that they drank because of boredom or because alcohol helped them escape their problems. This pattern of reasons for alcohol use is very similar to that given for marijuana use.

Trends in Alcohol-Related Behaviors

Recent trends in alcohol-related behaviors provide little cause for optimism regarding the current generation of American adolescents. For example, the percentages of 8th, 10th, and 12th graders who reported having been drunk at least once in the previous 12 months have not declined substantially within the past decade, but may, in fact, have increased in some age groups between 1992 and 1997. Similarly, the prevalence of another indicator of excessive adolescent drinking—heavy drinking (i.e., having five or more drinks in a row during the past 2 weeks)—appears to have increased among 12th graders in recent years, after declining consistently between 1982 and 1992. Conversely, two indicators of the beliefs and attitudes related to heavy drinking (i.e., disapproval of regular heavy drinking and the perception that heavy drinking is harmful) have declined since the early 1990s, after increasing during the 1980s. These findings suggest that a close association exists between adolescents' attitudes toward and beliefs about drinking and their alcohol-related behavior.

Implications for Public Policy

The findings presented in this article confirm that alcohol use and abuse, as well as alcohol-related problems, continue to be highly prevalent among American youth and a major source for concern. In fact, excessive alcohol use and its associated problems appear to have increased in recent years, following an earlier period during which both the rates of heavy drinking and the incidence of driving after drinking declined significantly among 12th graders. Moreover, the observations indicate that rates of alcohol use are equally high in almost all demographic subgroups. Finally, the beliefs and attitudes of adolescents toward drinking (and drinking and driving) show a close association with drinking behavior. What are the implications of these observations?

To date, researchers have not shown definitively whether changes in beliefs and attitudes actually play an active role in changing drinking behavior; whether changes in behavior produce changes in beliefs and attitudes about drinking; or whether other factors may affect beliefs, attitudes and behavior. Numerous analyses reported elsewhere, however, have supported the hypothesis that changes in attitudes and beliefs may have contributed to changes in the trends associated with both marijuana and cocaine use. It is therefore very likely that attitudes and beliefs similarly play an important role in determining alcohol-related behaviors. If beliefs and attitudes indeed have important causal roles in shaping behavior, the next question becomes, How can society elicit changes in those beliefs and attitudes? Various aspects of the larger culture, including the mass media and advertising, influence the prevailing attitudes and behaviors, although the extent of their contributions is still controversial.

> *"There is considerable evidence that alcohol use tends to precede use of illicit drugs."*

Alcohol-related public policies also help determine adolescent alcohol-use behaviors. For example, the increase in the minimum legal drinking age to 21 substantially reduced alcohol consumption as well as alcohol-related traffic fatalities among young Americans. Other policies that have been suggested to modify adolescent drinking behaviors include "zero tolerance" laws, restrictions on the hours of permitted sales and the density of alcohol outlets (e.g., liquor stores and restaurants), and making retail licenses contingent on not selling to minors. Finally, some researchers have asserted that raising alcohol taxes can significantly reduce adolescent drinking, although this hypothesis is still considered controversial.

The high levels of alcohol use and abuse, the recent disconcerting trends in these behaviors, and the erosion of antialcohol beliefs and attitudes among adolescents clearly indicate that more action is needed to address these problems on various fronts. Yet no consensus exists as to which specific actions should be undertaken. As more research results accumulate on the policies and programs aimed at deterring underage drinking, society's responses to the problem of underage drinking should become increasingly effective.

Underage Drinking Is America's Biggest Youth Drug Problem

by Elizabeth Shepard

About the author: *Elizabeth Shepard is a freelance journalist. The following essay is excerpted from a cover story she wrote for* Driven, *the magazine of Mothers Against Drunk Driving.*

Eighteen-year-old Leah Bean gave up alcohol in 1998. During her junior year in high school, Leah's best friend, April, was killed in a crash after leaving a party where kids had been drinking. The 19-year-old driver with whom April was riding crashed the car while driving with a blood alcohol content of .20 percent—more than twice the legal adult limit in Tennessee. According to Leah, the teens knew that party-goers were drinking and that the store which sold the teens alcohol was notorious for not checking IDs. But Leah echoes other teens' feelings of invincibility, admitting it is "as if there's a bubble around 15- to 21-year-olds that prevents bad things from happening."

Leah represents thousands of teenagers whose lives have been devastated by underage drinking. According to Monitoring the Future, a survey conducted by the University of Michigan, 31 percent of 12th-graders reported binge drinking (five or more drinks in a row) in the two weeks prior to the survey. Fifty-one percent reported consuming alcohol. Of eighth-graders, 15 percent reported binge drinking—and 24 percent consumed alcohol.

Alcohol Is Everywhere

In 1998, about 10.4 million drinkers in the United States were less than 21 years old. Sure, it's illegal, but that doesn't mean kids can't get their hands on alcohol.

In fact, 75 percent of young teens say that alcohol is easy to acquire. Approximately two-thirds of teenagers who drink report that they buy their own alcohol. Whether they buy it from stores or at bars that sell without carding, from

Excerpted from "America's No. 1 Youth Drug Problem," by Elizabeth Shepard, *Driven,* Fall 2000. Reprinted by permission of Mothers Against Drunk Driving.

home delivery services improperly monitored by state laws or from friends and siblings, alcohol is everywhere and easily within youths' reach.

The Lawrence County, Tennessee, MADD Youth In Action team conducted a study to see how many merchants sold alcohol to minors. Young men and women who were at least 21 years old but looked younger were sent into stores to try to purchase alcohol. The results were shocking: 48 percent of all salespeople never asked to see the buyers' identification. Of those sellers who asked, 50 percent of them sold the alcohol even after the buyers said they had no ID.

And it seems that underage drinkers make alcohol a priority in their budgets. Each year, college students spend approximately $5.5 billion on alcohol—more than they spend on soft drinks, milk, tea, coffee and books combined.

One 19-year-old college student, who wished to remain anonymous, said, "The drinking starts on Thursday nights and continues throughout the weekend. When one party runs out of alcohol, we all move on to another party. We drink until we can't drink another shot. Kids keep count of how many drinks they have each night; it's like a contest. When my parents send me my monthly check for living expenses, I make sure I save enough money to buy beer."

Teresa Robinson's 21-year-old daughter, Nicole, a college student, was killed in an alcohol-related crash November 13, 1997. "A group of kids went to a bar near campus to celebrate someone's 21st birthday, and they proceeded to get extremely drunk. Everyone at the bar knew that the kids were underage and drunk; but no one stopped them. The bartenders just kept serving everyone more drinks. I was stunned that no one in the bar tried to prevent the kids from getting in their cars."

Nicole was intoxicated when she got into the car being driven by a girl who was so drunk she fell on her face at the bar in front of the bartenders. The driver, with a blood alcohol content of .24 percent, was driving nearly 100 miles per hour when she crashed into a tree. The driver lived. Nicole died at the scene of the crash.

> *"By the time teenagers get to college . . . 4.4 million of them are binge drinkers."*

Teresa and her husband had cautioned Nicole never to drink and drive, and they never consumed any alcohol in front of their kids. "We were very conscientious about teaching our children about the dangers of alcohol. But I don't know how to get kids to listen. The media glorifies alcohol. The commercials are enticing. When kids get to college, it's a free-for-all—no one's watching them or saying yes or no. Kids who attended Nicole's funeral still drink and party and drive!"

Parents' Role

Many parents allow their teenage children to drink alcohol at home in an effort to teach them how to drink responsibly. They may have good intentions, but the results can be deadly. What they do, in fact, is facilitate their kids' comfort with alcohol, and the trouble only begins there.

"Kids don't know where to draw the line," Leah explained. "When parents open the door to alcohol for their kids, their kids figure if it's OK to drink at home, it's OK to drink out, too."

Many parents would be shocked to learn how young their children are when they begin to drink. Youth tend to begin drinking alcohol when they're as young as 12 years old. A new study shows a four-in-one chance that kids who begin drinking at 13 will become problem drinkers—and most likely impaired drivers—as opposed to young people who don't drink until the age of 21. By the time teenagers get to college, their rate of consumption has escalated dramatically: 4.4 million of them are binge drinkers and another 1.8 million are heavy drinkers (consuming five or more drinks on one occasion at least five times in the past month).

In some cases, parents aren't even aware that the underage and excessive drinking is taking place. A good example is spring break. Many parents send their kids off on trips to relax and play in the sun. Most often, these vacations are weeklong drinking junkets or "booze cruises" with excessive alcohol consumption.

> *"75 percent of young teens say that alcohol is easy to acquire."*

At the other extreme, parents sometimes acknowledge the drinking and help their teens plan parties hoping to ensure their safety by "controlling" their drinking environment. This was the case for teens from Highland Park, a wealthy Dallas suburb. Police broke up a warehouse party in Dallas and found that parents had rented the facility and contracted a bus company to safely deliver drunken high school students to and from the party.

But no matter how challenging parents may feel it is to communicate with their kids about alcohol, talking to them and setting clear boundaries are the most important things they can do. Survey after survey shows that young people rank parents among the top reasons for not using alcohol, demonstrating that parents have a great deal of impact and influence on their child's decision on whether to drink.

Laws holding parents liable for underage drinking incidents are becoming more common. It is evident that young people alone are not at the root of the underage drinking issue—adults often facilitate youth drinking by providing or buying the drinks.

Media's Mixed Messages

Even parents who set good examples and have discussed the rules regarding alcohol use have a tough battle. Advertisers—which spend more than $1 billion each year on alcohol advertisements alone—still portray alcohol as alluring and exciting for youth.

Whether via an advertisement or through careful product placement, images of alcohol in the media have become ubiquitous. A recent study funded by the Office of National Drug Control Policy (ONDCP) examined top-rated television network series broadcast between October and December 1998.

The results: alcohol was consumed in 71 percent of all episodes, including 65 percent of the programs most popular with teenagers. About one-

> *"The media glorifies alcohol."*

third of all the episodes were set in bars, nightclubs or restaurants where alcohol was consumed. Forty percent of the episodes made drinking look like a positive experience, while only 10 percent portrayed alcohol use negatively. Only one percent of the episodes portraying alcohol usage showed a refusal to use alcohol.

The Nationwide Cost of Its Most Menacing Drug

With happy hours, discounts on wine coolers and nickel-beer nights at bars near colleges, alcohol may be society's least expensive drug, but it is one of its most costly. Underage drinking costs the United States more than $58 billion every year—enough to buy every public school student a state-of-the-art computer.

Couple that with 1998 figures which calculate that alcohol-related traffic crashes cost this country $18,242,000,000 and you begin to see the devastating losses. But society pays a larger price than a monetary one. The death rate associated with youth alcohol use is staggering. Alcohol kills 6.5 times more youth than all other illicit drugs combined. The three leading causes of death for 15- to 24-year-olds are automobile crashes, homicides and suicides—alcohol is a leading factor in all three.

It would make sense, then, for the government to initiate and commit to a full-force effort to eradicate youth alcohol use. Surprisingly, when the federal government launched a five-year, $1 billion youth anti-drug media campaign, alcohol was excluded.

The Power of the Drug Alcohol

Alcohol itself and the powerful nature of its effects on young bodies is also a mighty force in America's No. 1 youth drug problem.

To put it simply, the effects of alcohol are seductive, potent and hazardous. Alcohol has absolutely no beneficial effects on teenagers, and its use needs to be taken seriously for what it is—perilous.

"Alcohol interacts with many different systems," explained Scott Swartzwelder, Ph.D., clinical professor at Duke University and author of *Buzzed: The Straight Dope About the Most Used and Abused Drugs from Alcohol to Ecstasy*. "It causes sedative effects and relieves anxiety, among other things. In teens, there is less of a sedative effect and that is dangerous and misleading for teens."

"The brain systems that give drinkers positive feelings may adapt to the alcohol and come to need it," Dr. Swartzwelder continued. "After repeated use, the brain systems come to feel that something is missing when alcohol is denied, and this motivates people to drink even more. Eventually, people drink to prevent the negative effects they feel from not drinking."

The adolescent brain is particularly susceptible to the powerful effects of the drug alcohol. "We know that alcohol consumption can impact learning and memory in the adolescent brain," Dr. Swartzwelder said. "The dangers and long-term consequences of alcohol use among teens are not fully understood."

A Silent Enemy, and a Deafening Need for Treatment

"Alcohol is the silent enemy," said Suzanne Smith, director of planning for operations at Phoenix House in Texas, the nation's leading substance abuse treatment, prevention and education organization. "Underage drinking remains a consistent problem. Society makes it accessible, and since it's legal for adults, the rules are confusing for adolescents. They don't really understand that alcohol is harmful to them."

In addition, alcohol is "the gateway drug" insofar as it's the precursor to teenagers trying many other types of substances. "Just about every kid who's being treated for drug abuse is mixing their drug of choice—be it marijuana or heroin or something else—with alcohol," said Smith.

"Alcohol kills 6.5 times more youth than all other illicit drugs combined."

According to Smith, "Most adolescents don't seek treatment on their own, and a parent, caretaker or more often than not the criminal justice system guides them to the help they need. Unfortunately, there are few long-term treatment programs available that provide teens with the structure they need to effect lasting changes in their behaviors, attitudes and values. As a result, only 10 percent of those who need help actually get it," so the problem can spiral out of control.

But treatment can work, and teenagers can be taught how to re-claim their lives by learning how bad alcohol really is for their bodies and for their future. "Treatment is really the second line of defense," Smith added. "Parents are unquestionably their children's first and most important teachers. They need to have heart-to-heart talks with their kids and give them accurate information about consequences of abusing alcohol and other substances."

Treatment is a win-win proposition: helping kids deal with their addiction and lead sober lives paves the way for them to become constructive, contributing citizens. And for every dollar society spends in treating addicted teens, it saves $12 on the criminal justice, health care and welfare systems.

First Steps for Alcohol-Free Youth

Greg Hamilton has been the chief of law enforcement of the Texas Alcohol Beverage Commission (TABC) for nearly seven years, and he said he's beginning to see a change nationwide.

"People in communities across the country are starting to get on board with this issue, but it takes time," he said.

"The TABC attacks the problem of underage drinking with a two-pronged approach: enforcement and education," he said. "We want to elicit voluntary compliance with the law by holding parents, kids, store owners and other adults responsible for giving or selling alcohol to minors. We take action against them and issue citations. We hold them accountable for their actions, and we educate them about the underage-drinking problem."

The TABC also educates law enforcement agents about the issue. "Law enforcement, like any other agency, is short staffed," Hamilton noted. "They used to tend to see underage drinking as a low priority, thinking that 'kids would be kids' and go through a drinking phase. But lately, police, store owners and parents are beginning to take the issue more seriously and doing something about it."

Still, more can be done. "Parents need to send a clear message that kids are not allowed to drink, and stop providing alcohol to their kids," he said. "High schools and colleges need to hold kids accountable for their actions when they buy or consume alcohol. And faith groups need to talk about the problem and educate the community."

Facing Reality

We can no longer point fingers at "bad kids" or negligent parents. Society as a whole bears the burden of the tragic consequences of underage drinking. MADD says that efforts to tackle the problem must involve parents—who, in their best efforts, can sometimes make uninformed and dangerous decisions. Retailers and the law enforcement community must strengthen their resolve to uphold the existing laws designed to protect young people. The media must be diligent in responsibly and accurately portraying the dangers of alcohol use by teens. Advertisers must cease targeting young people in marketing alcohol and alcohol-related products. Those who produce television shows and movies must take responsibility for the underage-drinking images they portray. Communities nationwide must provide treatment centers to help young people work their way back to alcohol-free lives. We must partner with youth.

"Alcohol has absolutely no beneficial effects on teenagers."

Youth have emerged as a major force in the efforts to tackle underage drinking. All across the nation, young people are banding together to put an end to America's No. 1 youth drug problem. They not only are taking action, they are making a difference.

By linking arm-in-arm with these young people, we can eradicate the nation's most devastating youth drug problem—alcohol.

The Problem of Underage Drinking Is Too Often Ignored

by Mathea Falco

About the author: *Mathea Falco is president of Drug Strategies, a nonprofit research institute. He was assistant secretary of state for international narcotics matters from 1977 to 1981.*

Recent tragedies such as the death of a 20-year-old Georgetown student following a drunken fight and other tales of alcohol-related arrests and accidents have opened many parents' eyes to the problem of binge drinking on college campuses. But too many parents fail to realize that excessive drinking often begins much earlier.

Alcohol Is Kids' Drug of Choice

Alcohol is the drug of choice among high school and middle school students today. And while one-third of high school students say they have binged on alcohol in the past month, a Peter Hart poll found that just 3 percent of high school students' parents think their teens have done so. This awareness gap has serious consequences for today's youth. Alcohol, especially among youth, is taking a real toll.

Parents are not alone in underestimating the problem of teen drinking. Teen drinking costs more than $58 billion annually, including costs from traffic accidents, violent crime, suicide attempts and treatment. Yet the federal government has invested little in the problem and has no comprehensive strategy to address alcohol-related problems. One of the government's largest drug prevention initiatives—the Office of National Drug Control Policy's anti-drug media campaign—is aimed at preventing illicit drug use among young people. But no comparable program exists for the much larger problem of underage drinking.

We can do better. We owe it to our children.

Reprinted, with the permission of the author, from "Alcohol: Kids' Drug of Choice," by Mathea Falco, *Washington Post*, May 27, 2000.

According to a recent Drug Strategies report, "Millennium Hangover," regular drinking among teens surpasses regular use of all illicit drugs combined. And teens are getting drunk more often than in the past. In 1998, one in three high school seniors reported being drunk in the preceding month—up 13 percent since 1993.

When teens begin drinking at an early age, they greatly increase their risk for serious alcohol problems later in life. According to the National Institute on Alcohol Abuse and Alcoholism, teens who drink before age 15 are four times more likely to develop alcohol dependence than those who begin drinking at age 21.

And underage drinkers are much more likely to participate in other risky behaviors, such as unprotected sex and other drug use. The more teens drink, the more likely they are to drink and drive, or to ride in a car where the driver has been drinking. Young drinkers also smoke more often than those who do not drink.

Underestimating the Problem

Until parents, teachers and policymakers face up to the realities of underage drinking, kids will fail to get the message about the dangers of alcohol. Despite the higher number of accidents and deaths associated with alcohol use, teens believe that alcohol is less dangerous than other drugs. Almost half of teenagers view illicit drugs as the biggest problem facing their generation, while less than 10 percent cite alcohol.

And it is far too easy for teens to get alcohol. Nearly 90 percent of 10th-graders say that alcohol is easy to get, whether from older friends and siblings, a parent's liquor cabinet, licensed alcohol outlets or even over the Internet.

Americans have long focused on the devastating effects of illicit drugs on this country's health and safety. Underage drinking rarely provokes similar concern. That needs to change. It is time that the prevention of teen drinking becomes as high a national priority as preventing teen smoking and other drug use.

Parents must begin much earlier to talk with their children about the dangers of drinking. Enforcement of the minimum drinking age must improve. And the federal government must finally stare down the alcohol lobby and make a significant investment in preventing underage drinking.

The drinking habits teenagers form in high school, and sometimes earlier, are sure to get worse when students begin to enjoy the freedom of a college campus. In fact, a recent Harvard School of Public Health study found that despite years of aggressive prevention efforts, frequent heavy

> *"It is time that the prevention of teen drinking becomes as high a national priority as preventing teen smoking and other drug use."*

drinking among college students is on the rise. The study's findings and the constant stream of disasters that result from teen alcohol abuse should be a wake-up call for parents and policymakers. It's time to get serious.

Binge Drinking on College Campuses Is a Serious Problem

by Susan Resneck Pierce

About the author: *Susan Resneck Pierce, president of the University of Puget Sound, serves on the National Advisory Council Subcommittee on College Drinking of the National Institute on Alcohol Abuse and Alcoholism.*

Shortly after returning home from a National Institute on Alcohol and Alcohol Abuse (NIAAA) meeting on college drinking, I learned that a student from my own campus had been cited for creating a public disturbance. He argued that he and his friends were simply being college students.

Irresponsible drinking on the part of young people has been a problem literally for centuries. For example, Homer describes its devastating effects in "The Odyssey." What is different today is that many students drink to get drunk and many young women join their male classmates in drinking to excess. The problem is aggravated by America's dependence on the automobile.

Unfortunately, college students are not the only ones in denial about the negative effects of excessive drinking.

Administrators and faculty also look away from the alcohol-reliance of some students and have unwittingly helped create campus cultures in which students drink excessively without suffering significant consequences.

Troubling Statistics

The problem is serious. Although most college students drink moderately or abstain, a recent Harvard School of Public Health study reports that 42 percent had at least one excessive drinking episode (i. e., more than five consecutive drinks for men and more than four for women) in the two-week period prior to the survey and 21 percent had three or more such excessive drinking episodes in that same period.

Reprinted from "College Drinking: The Elephant on Campus," by Susan Resneck Pierce, *Seattle Times*, January 31, 2000, by permission of the author.

Another recent study at 113 colleges and universities concludes that alcohol abuse is responsible for 64 percent of campus incidents of violent behavior, 42 percent of physical injuries, two-thirds of all property damage and close to 40 percent of both emotional and academic difficulties.

The Department of Education reports that 84 college students have died since 1996 because of alcohol but suggests this is a low estimate.

Valuing education, knowledge and reason, colleges have assumed that teaching students about the negative consequences of excessive drinking would change behavior. But when it comes to alcohol abuse, education alone is not enough. We also have not assessed our programs and so are devoting lots of time, energy and resources into programs that are not or may not be effective.

College Drinking Is Entrenched

Changing this alcohol-reliant culture will not be easy for at least the following reasons:

Some students equate alcohol with their rite of passage into adulthood and see it as a personal right, even if they are underage.

Some students turn to alcohol as a social lubricant, leading such groups as athletes and fraternity members to drink excessively because their peers do.

Students believe that other students drink more than they do and so in turn drink more than they might otherwise. (Norms-based programs that educate students about the actual levels of drinking of peers have had some success in reducing drinking.)

Advertising and alcohol promotions at bars and clubs promote drinking. At a private university club in New York, I recently was struck that flyers promoting alcohol nights were adjacent to those announcing events for prospective students.

On many campuses, grade inflation, diminished faculty expectations, Fridays without classes and few early morning classes enable students to drink with impunity. When the gentleman's C is replaced with the gentleperson's B+, students without self-discipline or motivation can develop respectable transcripts.

Raising the drinking age from 18 to 21 has reduced both automobile fatalities and underage drinking. The law has, however, forced campuses to deal with the ethical and legal dilemma of trying simultaneously to enforce the law and, to save lives, to encourage underage students to drink responsibly.

Colleges and universities must have the courage to confront this serious problem, which in one way or another affects all our students.

To reduce alcohol abuse will require campuses across the country to act carefully and deliberately, with the clear goal not just of educating students but more importantly of changing their behavior. It will require all of us, both on our campuses and in our local communities, to move beyond denial about excessive drinking.

But most of all, it will require us to disabuse our students and our communities of the notion that drinking really is just part of students being students.

The Extent of Underage Drinking Is Exaggerated

by David J. Hanson

About the author: *David J. Hanson is a professor of sociology at the State University of New York at Potsdam and the author of* Alcohol Education: What We Must Do.

"College Students of America Wade Deeper Into Sea of Booze"

"Students Major in Binging"

"College Binge Drinking Soars"

We've all seen these or similar distressing headlines. Case in point—newspapers across the country carried frightening statistics reported by Joe Califano and the Center on Addiction and Substance Abuse (CASA).

On national television programs, Califano reported horror stories of alcohol abuse among college students, associating it with assault, rape, and even murder. A CASA report asserted that

"60 percent of college women who have acquired sexually transmitted diseases, including AIDS and genital herpes, were under the influence of alcohol at the time they had intercourse."

"90 percent of all reported campus rapes occur when alcohol is being used by either the assailant or the victim."

"The number of women who reported drinking to get drunk more than tripled between 1977 and 1993."

"95 percent of violent crime on campus is alcohol-related."

Bogus Statistics

But relax. These assertions are not supported by the facts. According to an investigative reporter [Kathy McNamara-Meis], one of these statistics "appears to have been pulled from thin air," another is based on no evidence whatsoever,

Excerpted from "Underage Drinking," by David J. Hanson, published at www2.potsdam.edu/alcohol-info. Reprinted with permission from the author.

another is based on one inadequate survey and is inconsistent with all other surveys, and a fourth is highly suspect at best.

Even the most improbable of statistics are often repeated by news media as fact and become part of public belief. It is now commonly believed that the average young person will have seen 100,000 beer commercials between the age of two and eighteen. But just think—sixteen years or about 5,844 days occur between a person's second and eighteenth birthday. To see 100,000 beer commercials in that period, a person would have to see an average of more than seventeen a day! Common sense alone should have been enough to dispel the myth. But this clearly absurd statistic has been gullibly repeated over and over. . . .

Distorted, biased, or incorrect statistics may attract media attention. They may even influence public policy. But they can't contribute to a reduction of alcohol abuse, which requires accurate information and unbiased interpretation. Therefore, we must be skeptical of surprising, sensationalized statistics.

Typically, inflated statistics are associated with talk of epidemics, threats to our youth, and similar alarmist language. Often they are promoted by groups with laudable sounding names such as the Center for Science in the Public Interest. But many such groups, which may have underlying social or political agendas, tend to exaggerate the extent and growth of problems in which they have a vested interest and, typically, a proposed solution. Problems widely seen by the public as being of epidemic proportion justify ever larger budgets, increased staffs, higher salaries, more power, and greater organizational prestige.

And many groups and individuals have a vested interest in exaggerating the extent of drinking problems. They generally include federal, state, and other governmental alcohol agencies; private alcohol agencies; alcohol treatment facilities, therapists, alcohol educators; and often alcohol abusers themselves.

Accentuating the Negative

Editors sometimes confess that sensational statistics have much more reader appeal than reports of generally declining problems. Thus, when alcohol statistics are presented by researchers, the media tend to spin stories in a negative light. For example, the *Wall Street Journal* ran the following headline and lead sentence in response to a press release by the Harvard School of Public Health:

"BINGE" DRINKING AT NATION'S COLLEGES IS WIDESPREAD, A
HARVARD STUDY FINDS

Boston – Almost half of all students surveyed at 140 U.S. colleges admitted to "binge" drinking, leading from fights to vandalism. . . .

Instead, the study could have resulted in this headline and lead story:

MAJORITY OF COLLEGE STUDENTS DRINK MODERATELY OR NOT
AT ALL, A HARVARD STUDY FINDS

Boston – More than half of all students surveyed at 140 U.S. colleges report moderate drinking as the campus norm, resulting in relatively small numbers (only 9 percent) who get hurt or vandalize. . . .

Similarly, a nation-wide survey of students at 168 U. S. colleges and universities found that:

- 98% have never been in trouble with a college administrator because of behavior resulting from drinking too much,
- 93% have never received a lower grade because of drinking too much,
- 93% have never come to class after having had several drinks, and
- 90% have never damaged property, pulled a false alarm, or engaged in similar inappropriate behavior because of drinking.

While headlines typically express alarm over drinking epidemics among collegians, in reality drinking among college students continues to decline as abstaining from alcohol climbs:

- The proportion of college students who abstain from alcohol jumped 58% between 1983 and 1994, according to a series of nation-wide surveys.
- A 16% increase in college non-drinkers has been found between the periods of 1989–1991 and 1995–1997 by the federally-funded CORE Institute.
- A recent study by Dr. Henry Wechsler of Harvard University found that the proportion of collegiate abstainers in the U.S. jumped nearly 22% in the four years since his earlier study.
- The proportion of non-drinkers among college students in the U.S. recently reached a record-breaking all-time high according to statistics collected for the National Institute on Drug Abuse by

> *"When alcohol statistics are presented by researchers, the media tend to spin stories in a negative light."*

the Institute for Social Research of the University of Michigan. That means that *the proportion of students who drink has dropped to an all-time record-breaking low!*

- The proportion of first year college students who drink beer has fallen dramatically and recently reached the lowest level in 30 years, according to national annual surveys by UCLA's Higher Education Research Institute. Similar drops were found for wine and distilled spirits.

So-called binge drinking among American college students also continues to decline For example, the proportion of college students who binge decreased significantly within a recent four-year period, according to the Harvard University study mentioned above.

These findings are consistent with data collected by for the National Institute on Drug Abuse by the Institute for Social Research. The ISR found that *college "binge" drinking in the U.S. recently reached the lowest level* of the entire 17-year period that its surveys have been conducted.

College students "simply don't drink as much as everyone seems to think they do," according to researchers who used Breathalizers at the University of North Carolina at Chapel Hill. Even on the traditional party nights of Thursday, Friday and Saturday, 66% of the students returned home with absolutely *no* blood alcohol content; two of every three students had not a trace of alcohol in their systems at the end of party nights.

"I'm not surprised at all by these results," said Rob Foss, manager of Alcohol Studies for the UNC Highway Traffic Safety Center, which conducted the study with funding from the National Highway Traffic Safety Administration and the North Carolina Governor's Highway Safety Program. "Other Breathalizer studies we have done with drivers and recreational boaters show similar results—less drinking than is generally believed. We have substantial misperceptions about alcohol use in this country."

> *"Within a period of 17 years, there has been a 13% decrease in the proportion of American high school students who have ever consumed alcohol."*

Similarly, drinking among young people in general continues to decline. For example, the proportion of youths aged 12 through 17 who consumed any alcohol within the previous month has dropped from 50% in 1979 down to 19% in 1998, according to the federal government's *National Household Survey on Drug Abuse*. That's down from one of every two youths to fewer than one of every five.

The proportion of both junior and senior high school students who have consumed any alcohol during the year has dropped again for the third year in a row, according to the PRIDE Survey, a nation-wide study of 138,079 students, which is designated by federal law as an official measure of substance use by teen-agers in the U.S.

Within a period of 17 years, there has been a 13% decrease in the proportion of American high school seniors who have ever consumed alcohol and a *24% decrease in the proportion who have ever "binged."*

These are very important facts, but you probably haven't seen or heard much, if anything, about them in the mass media.

A Better Approach

In spite of all the hype and exaggeration, the fact remains that alcohol abuse is still a significant problem among youth that requires our attention. Thus, the question remains: what can we do to reduce alcohol abuse?

Significantly, hype and exaggeration are actually an important part of the problem. A negative spin on drinking statistics has a negative impact on drinking behaviors by contributing to a "reign of error." When people believe that "everyone is doing it," abusive drinking increases as they try to conform to the imagined behaviors of others. This is especially true among young people. Perceptions of the drinking behaviors of others strongly influences the actual drinking behavior of students.

The exaggeration of alcohol abuse tends to create a self-fulfilling prophesy.

The more young people believe heavy drinking occurs, the more heavily they tend to drink in order to conform. Research has demonstrated that reducing misperceptions of alcohol abuse is an effective way to reduce actual abuse among adolescents.

Individual students almost always believe that most others on campus drink more heavily than they do and the disparity between the perceived and the actual behaviors tend to be quite large. By conducting surveys of actual behavior and publicizing the results, the extent of heavy drinking can be quickly and significantly reduced. The most carefully assessed such project demonstrated a 35% reduction in heavy drinking, a 31% reduction in alcohol-related injuries to self, and a 54% reduction in alcohol-related injuries to others.

This approach to reducing alcohol problems is remarkably quick and inexpensive and has proven to be highly effective.

Teen Alcohol Education Programs Exaggerate the Dangers of Drinking

by Stanton Peele

About the author: *Stanton Peele is a psychologist and researcher specializing in drug and alcohol addiction and the author of* The Diseasing of America: How We Allowed Recovery Zealots and the Treatment Industry to Convince Us We Are Out of Control.

"Efforts to curb excessive drinking on college campuses fall short," newspaper headlines screamed. Henry Wechsler, director of the College Alcohol Studies Program at the Harvard School of Public Health, has been studying binge drinking on U.S. campuses since 1993. By 1999, he found, the percentage of student who frequently binged had not declined, but increased, as had the number of abstainers.

This split or alternation between abstinence and binge drinking is an old one. It is characteristic of cultures which view alcohol as a tempting evil. From this perspective, drinking must be avoided. However, once tasted, it cannot be resisted.

This contrasts with those cultures (most notably Mediterranean, Jewish, and Chinese), where alcohol is seen as an ordinary part of religious or social celebrations. As one researcher described drinking in New York's Chinatown: "The children drank, and they soon learned a set of attitudes that attended the practice. While drinking was socially sanctioned, becoming drunk was not. The individual who lost control of himself under the influence of liquor was ridiculed and, if he persisted in his defection, ostracized."

The Failure of Alcohol Education Programs

The continuing high rate of bingeing on campuses is particularly disturbing given the tremendous efforts devoted to campus alcohol education programs. Wechsler's reaction: "My disappointment is, given all the action on college

Reprinted from "A National Failure at Moderation," by Stanton Peele, published at *The Stanton Peele Addiction Web Site* (www.peele.net), April 1, 2000. Reprinted by permission of the author.

campuses to deal with this problem . . . , the fact that it has stayed so remarkably stable shows what a difficult problem it is."

Of what do these educational programs consist? Primarily, they aim to eliminate all drinking on campus. That is, rather than encouraging moderation, the message is that alcohol is bad. These programs cite statistic after statistic about the dangers of drinking—drunk driving, risky sex, cirrhosis.

But listing only negative consequences from drinking became more difficult when epidemiologic studies

> *"Rather than encouraging moderation, the message [of teen alcohol programs] is that alcohol is bad."*

of large populations discovered that drinking also often conveys benefits. Long-term studies of 85,000 nurses conducted at Harvard, and of a half million adults age 30 and older conducted by the American Cancer Society, found that moderate drinkers lived longer on average than nondrinkers. Since the vast majority of the drinkers surveyed drank lightly or moderately, these benefits hold for most adult drinkers.

But American public health does not do well at conveying the idea that drinking is a double-edged activity, one with potential benefits as well as real dangers, and that moderation is the distinguishing feature between the two. Take American high school students. Each year, seniors are surveyed by the University of Michigan about their drinking practices and attitudes.

In 1999, three quarters of the seniors had drunk alcohol over the previous year. Disturbingly, more than half had gotten drunk—a third had been drunk in the prior month. But what is strangest about this cohort is their views on drinking. Although they frequently drink to excess, they condemn such drinking—64% say they disapprove of adults who "Have five or more drinks once or twice each weekend."

Remarkably, however, even more (69%) disapprove of adults who "Take one or two drinks nearly every day." Yet this is exactly the type of drinking which leads to the fewest negative outcomes, and which is most likely to extend a drinker's life span!

American education programs seemingly fail to convey the complexities of alcohol's effects. Consider the reactions to the revelation that binge drinking continues unabated on college campuses. In a parallel effort to the Harvard college drinking research, the Robert Wood Johnson Foundation has been addressing binge drinking at 10 universities.

More Abstinence, More Binging

The result of the Johnson Foundation efforts? More abstinence and more bingeing. Rather than seeing this bifurcation as problematic, Richard Yoast, director of the program, claims the program has been positive. Dr. Yoast noted with approval that the number of students who were abstaining on the targeted campuses had almost doubled since 1993, while the rates of heavy drinking were rising *more slowly* than the national average.

Mary Sue Coleman is president of the University of Iowa, which is part of the Johnson Foundation study. Remarking on continuing binge drinking at her school, Dr. Coleman vowed to stop serving alcohol at her own pre-football game brunches.

Were her guests getting drunk? It seems unlikely. But, like many other Americans, Dr. Coleman sees all drinking as problematic. Somehow, the United States finds it hard to escape its temperance roots and to steer a middle course with alcohol.

Not All Underage Drinking Is Harmful

by Dwight B. Heath

About the author: *Dwight B. Heath is a professor of anthropology at Brown University and the author of* Drinking Occasions: Comparative Perspectives on Alcohol and Culture.

Early in 2000 the American print media amply reported another in a long trail of negative announcements regarding alcoholic-beverage consumption. The press release that had triggered this wave of alcohol reportage, with its somber extrapolations, had grown out of a research project sponsored by the U.S. National Institute on Alcohol Abuse and Alcoholism (NIAAA). This study, published in the *Journal of Substance Abuse*, had concerned the correlation of (1) age of first beverage alcohol intake and (2) alcoholism. Its principal finding was, in simple terms, that subjects who had first imbibed at an early age were, to a statistically significant degree, likelier eventually to become alcoholics than were those who hadn't.

It is no secret that correlation often has little bearing on causation, yet many print journalists treated this finding as if it were dramatic proof that alcoholic beverage consumption is highly addictive and that it is dangerous for anyone under age 21. The same finding might be counterintuitive to anyone conversant with life in modern Europe or among Orthodox Jews. In Europe, frequently individuals are first invited to drink at an early age, but rates of alcohol dependence tend to be very low. Orthodox Jewish males are commonly given a taste of wine on the occasion of their circumcision—eight days after their birth. And many followers of that faith—youngsters as well as adults—drink wine ceremonially at least twice a week. But rates of drinking-related problems among Orthodox Jews are remarkably low.

Indeed, the NIAAA finding does not apply in most parts of the world outside the United States—where, alas, the finding is altogether reasonable. At least some of the efforts of the new temperance movement—i.e., the efforts of a

Reprinted from "Should We 'Just Say No' to Childhood Drinking?" by Dwight B. Heath, *Priorities*, vol. 12, no. 2, (2000). Reprinted by permission of the American Council on Science and Health.

loose, variegated coalition of activists trying to reduce beverage-alcohol consumption by humans categorically—evidently have been counterproductive.

Childhood drinking is deviant in the U.S.; in many states it is also illegal. One would reasonably expect that in such a setting underage drinkers would consist almost entirely of persons who freely behave in other deviant (e.g., risky or illegal) ways, in some cases deliberately. By the same token, one would reasonably expect that law-abiding, conformist youngsters who tend to avoid risks would also tend to defer drinking at least until adulthood. In other words, it is almost certainly not adolescent or childhood drinking per se that leads to adulthood drinking problems; it is far likelier that factors that predispose children and adolescents to deviant drinking and to other such behaviors are responsible.

The New Temperance Movement

Yet advocates of the new temperance movement have structured the relationship in the U.S. between childhood drinking and adulthood drinking problems so that the former phenomenon appears almost always to result in the latter!

In most parts of the world, beverage alcohol lacks the "forbidden fruit" appeal that invites its use by youngsters as a demonstration of maturity and/or as a means of becoming sociable, sexy, dynamic, or more powerful. Where children are not "protected from alcohol," their behavior suggests no need for such protection. These children take up drinking in relatively supportive surroundings (usually in their homes and among adult members of their families) as a wholesome and enjoyable part of everyday life—rather than as an illicit, surreptitious consequence of peer pressure.

> *"In Europe, frequently individuals are first invited to drink at an early age, but rates of alcohol dependence tend to be very low."*

As an anthropologist, I often deal with patterns of populations that are small, isolated, or tribal and whose characteristic beliefs and behaviors would not be feasible in industrial or post-industrial communities. But some of the best illustrations of my case concern the present-day middle classes of France, Italy, Spain, and other developed countries. Through official statistics from such countries, on such well-studied communities, I have repeatedly demonstrated that the incidence of so-called alcohol-related problems (physiological, psychological, social, economic, etc.) is inversely related both to "age of onset" (i.e., how early in one's life one first imbibes) and to average per capita consumption of beverage alcohol. This is just the opposite of what is claimed by the World Health Organization, the NIAAA, and other organizations primarily concerned with restricting alcoholic-beverage availability as a public health policy.

The same climate that almost guarantees that underage American drinkers will be otherwise deviant and will flout the law also virtually ensures that they will often drink furtively and excessively or rashly, and that they will do so among peers ignorant or unmindful of the specific long- and short-term risks of alcohol abuse—peers who may be reluctant to summon an adult in the event of an acute problem.

The "Just Say No" approach thus invites troubles.

In Most Cultures Underage Drinking Is Not a Problem

In communities in which early socialization to drinking is the norm (i.e., in most communities), youngsters learn simultaneously how to drink moderately, how and why to avoid drunkenness, that drinking will not magically improve one's personality, and that excessive drinking illustrates weakness.

In short, the theory that early drinking leads to drinking problems is correct—but only in those few communities in which the normative and legal systems make the theory correct.

For anyone for whom such cross-cultural evidence is not compelling, I recommend reading an article whose authors used a statistical methodology similar to that used by most of those who publish in support of the above-mentioned theory: "Age at First Drink and Risk for Alcoholism: A Noncausal Association," published in the prestigious journal *Alcoholism: Clinical and Experimental Research.*

Chapter 2

What Problems Are Associated with Teen Alcohol Abuse?

Chapter Preface

For teens, the most immediate physical problem associated with alcohol abuse is the possibility of alcohol poisoning, which can cause blackouts, vomiting, and sometimes even death. Hangovers are a less dangerous, but nevertheless painful, side effect of binge drinking. In the long term, the possibility of becoming an alcoholic is perhaps the most serious medical problem associated with chronic alcohol abuse.

There are also many social problems associated with teen alcohol abuse. These are problems that occur because of the irresponsible and antisocial behavior many people exhibit when they are inebriated. Drunk driving is a well-known example. Rates of drunk driving are highest among teens, in part because their youth and inexperience with alcohol makes them more likely to use poor judgment after drinking.

A less publicized problem associated with teen drinking is the link between alcohol abuse and violent crime. Alcohol abuse greatly increases an individual's likelihood of committing—or becoming a victim of—violence. According to the U.S. Department of Justice, roughly 37 percent of sexual assaults and 27 percent of aggravated assaults involve offenders that have been drinking. Alcohol-related violence is a serious problem among teens. Nearly 9 percent of the perpetrators of alcohol-related violence, and over 13 percent of the victims, are under age 21. Early alcohol abuse is associated with criminal behavior in general. About one-half of all juveniles in some type of correctional facilities were under the influence of drugs or alcohol at the time they committed the offense, and about 20 percent of state prisoners describe themselves as daily drinkers and report that they began drinking before age 17.

Violence is just one of the social problems associated with the irresponsible use of alcohol. The authors in the following chapter explore other harmful consequences of teen alcohol abuse, including poor performance in school, an increased risk of contracting a sexually transmitted disease, and the tragic consequences of drunk driving among youth.

Underage Drinking Can Lead to Alcoholism

by the *Omaha World-Herald*

About the author: *The following viewpoint was published as a staff editorial in the* Omaha World-Herald, *a prominent midwestern newspaper.*

[In January 1997] John Gregory Dunne wrote perceptively in *The New Yorker* magazine about an underclass of young people in southeastern Nebraska who worked in dead-end jobs or not at all, living mostly to party on evenings and weekends.

They would earn a few dollars, get drunk and sometimes turn to petty crime. Dunne found them when he was in Nebraska to tell the story of the slaying of Teena Brandon and two companions in a farmhouse near Humboldt, for which one young man now sits on death row and another is serving a life term in prison.

At the center of the story was alcohol. The two men were drunk when they raped Brandon, a woman posing as a man, in 1993. They were drunk over much of the four-day period when they plotted her death. And they were drunk that New Year's Eve, when they murdered her and two companions. John Lotter, who faces the electric chair, and Marvin Nissen were barely more than 20 when they committed the murders. Their victims were all in their early 20s. As Dunne's article made clear, alcohol dominated their lifestyle—indeed, their life.

Teen Drinking and Alcoholism

Such evil, of course, can't be blamed entirely on alcohol, though the desultory meaninglessness and emptiness of the lives of all the characters in the Teena Brandon morality play may be both the cause and the effect of teen drinking—one of the most serious social problems in this or any other part of the country.

A new study reveals even more reasons to be concerned. Conducted by the National Institute on Alcohol Abuse and Alcoholism, it indicated that teen-agers who drink before they are old enough to drive have more than a 40 percent

Reprinted, with permission, from "That First Drink Can Begin a Life of Misery or Crime," editorial, *Omaha World-Herald*, January 17, 1998.

chance of becoming alcoholics during their lifetime.

The study didn't include just underage drinkers who regularly got smashed. It included kids who were given a giggly sip from Dad's glass of beer or wine—something many children are permitted to do.

That is an appalling statistic. It should alarm every parent who has ever winked or chuckled when his or her teen-ager had an illicit beer. It should cause regret to every youth club leader, teacher or other adult who has known about a kegger or a beer blast and didn't do something about it.

The study was touted as the largest alcohol survey ever conducted. Researchers asked 42,000 adults when they began drinking. They found that more than 43 percent of people who began drinking before age 14 developed alcoholism later. Another 10 percent of those people abused alcohol without being classified as full-fledged alcoholics, the study suggested.

> *"Teen-agers who drink before they are old enough to drive have more than a 40 percent chance of becoming alcoholics during their lifetime."*

Of the people who waited until they were 21 or 22 to drink, about 10 percent developed into alcoholics. The chances of developing alcoholism dropped by 14 percent each year a person delayed drinking, the researchers said.

Researchers were unable to explain the results. Bridget Grant, one of the authors, and Enoch Gordis, director of the institute, suggested that younger brains may be more sensitive to alcohol. Perhaps, they speculated, older people simply have better things to do—family and career, for instance.

Wasted Lives

Whatever the reason, the statistic suggests that young Nebraskans face deadly problems when they begin drinking young, as many of them do. Some will grow up to live lives dedicated to the obtaining and consuming of alcohol. Some will die from the effects of addiction.

Most will not plot and commit murder. But in some cases—in far too many cases if the institute's study is correct—they will waste a substantial portion of their lives on alcohol. Because their parents were unwilling or unable to stop them. Because someone old enough to know better bought them a drink or some clerk who should have been more conscientious didn't check their ID. Because the messages drilled into them by don't-drink programs and lessons and public service announcements had little effect.

Because they began drinking far too young and no one prevented it.

Underage Drinking Contributes to Drunk Driving Fatalities

by the National Highway Traffic Safety Administration

About the author: *The National Highway Traffic Safety Administration is a division of the U.S. Department of Transportation responsible for reducing deaths, injuries, and economic losses resulting from motor vehicle crashes.*

The rate that young people died in alcohol-related crashes reached an historic low in 1998. For every 100,000 youth, ages 15 through 20, nine died in a crash where a driver or non-occupant had been drinking. The one-point reduction from 1997 to 1998 occurred primarily because the youth population increased by over a half million while the number of fatalities remained relatively stable (there were only eight fewer fatalities). For comparison purposes, in the early 1980s the alcohol-related fatality rate was consistently around twenty. What this means is that the odds of a teenager dying in an alcohol-related crash is half what it used to be fifteen years ago.

The specific causes for this reduction are unclear but there were a number of identifiable events that we believe contributed to this reduction in youth deaths. The early eighties saw the rise of the citizen activist groups that focused on drunk driving, particularly RID (Remove Intoxicated Drivers), MADD (Mothers Against Drunk Driving) and SADD (Students Against Driving Drunk, now Students Against Destructive Decisions). The early eighties saw the creation of the Presidential Commission Against Drunk Driving and its successor, the National Commission Against Drunk Driving. All this activity led to legislation, most important of which in the youth area was the increase in the drinking age and the lowering of illegal blood alcohol content (BAC) for young drivers. Every state has now set 21 as the legal purchase and public possession age for alcoholic beverages and, at most, a .02 BAC limit for drivers under age 21. These two laws alone have saved thousands upon thousands of lives—of all ages.

Reprinted from *1998 Youth Fatal Crash and Alcohol Facts*, by the National Highway Traffic Safety Administration, published at www.nhtsa.dot.gov/people/injury/alcohol/Fatal1998Y/toc.html.

The Ongoing Challenge

Reducing teenage alcohol-related fatalities will be increasingly more difficult to achieve with a rising youth population. There are a number of things that must be done. They include reaching the parents who look the other way or ignore drinking by their underage children; increasing enforcement of the laws that have been shown to be effective in reducing fatalities; getting treatment for those hard to reach young people that are alcoholics or have drinking problems; and convincing young people that underage drinking, in addition to drinking and driving, is socially unacceptable.

Our challenge is twofold: continue to reduce the youth alcohol-related crash rate, irrespective of the size of the population, and to achieve a decline in the actual number of young people that die in these crashes.

Each [statistic in this viewpoint] represents real people, sons and daughters, brothers and sisters, whose deaths have devastated friends and family members. Our ultimate goal is to make teenage alcohol-related fatalities a rare event.

The data contained in this report focus on alcohol-related fatal crashes involving young people, ages 15 through 20, from 1982 to 1998. The data selected to illustrate this problem primarily fall into four categories:

- *Youth Fatalities.* Those who died in motor vehicle crashes (drivers, passengers, or non-occupants) who were 15 to 20 years old. An "alcohol-related" fatality occurs if any driver or non-occupant (i.e., pedestrian or bicyclist) involved in the crash had been drinking (i.e., their BAC was greater than zero). The young person killed, therefore, may or may not have been drinking.
- *Young Drivers Involved in Fatal Crashes.* 15-to-20-year-old drivers involved in a crash that resulted in a fatality. These drivers may have been fatally injured in the crash or survived the crash and the fatality may have been a youth, a child (under age 15) or an adult.
- *Young Drivers Killed.* 15-to-20-year-old drivers who were killed in a motor vehicle crash.
- *Youth Fatalities by Involvement of Young Drivers.* Youths who were killed in a motor vehicle crash in which a young person was driving. The fatality could have been the driver, a passenger, or a non-occupant 15 to 20 years old.

The young driver (also aged 15 through 20) involved in the crash may or may not have been "at fault" and may or may not have been drinking.

The data in these four categories are broken out by alcohol-related

"Our ultimate goal is to make teenage alcohol-related fatalities a rare event."

(A/R) involvement, which is estimated by National Highway Traffic Safety Administration (NHTSA). If a fatality is alcohol-related, a driver or non-occupant had a measurable blood alcohol content (BAC). The alcohol involvement is further broken down to indicate if the BAC was between .01 and .09 percent or if it was equal to or greater than .10 percent, which is over the legal limit for adult drivers in all States. (It should be noted that, as of June 1998, all States and the District of Columbia have set lower BAC limits for drivers under the age of 21 at .02 or lower.). . .

Youth Crash Fatalities Ages 15 Through 20

- Over one-third of all deaths for people ages 15 to 20 result from motor vehicle crashes (Vital Statistics Mortality Data -1997, CDC). In 1998, over one-third of these motor vehicle fatalities involved alcohol. Nearly two-thirds of the young motor vehicle occupant fatalities did not use a seat belt or motorcycle helmet.

Trends

"Over one-third of all deaths for people ages 15 to 20 result from motor vehicle crashes."

- The population of the United States, ages 15 through 20, has decreased from 24.3 million in 1982 to 23.3 million in 1998—a decrease of 4.1 percent. During this same time period, motor vehicle fatalities for this age group decreased by over 27 percent, while alcohol-related fatalities decreased by almost 59 percent.
- Since 1989, less than half of youth motor vehicle fatalities have been alcohol-related. Drinking and driving is no longer the leading cause of death for teenagers. However, motor vehicle crashes remain so.
- The alcohol-related traffic fatality rate for youth has been cut by over half since 1988—from 19 to 9 deaths per 100,000 youth. The rate in 1998 was the lowest since record-keeping began in 1982.
- Over 2,000 fewer young people died in traffic crashes in 1998 than in 1988, a 26 percent reduction. Alcohol-related fatalities dropped by almost 50 percent in the past decade.
- In 1998, alcohol-related fatalities for youth decreased by 0.4 percent since 1997, only 8 fewer deaths.
- 2,210 youth died in alcohol-related crashes in 1998—35.8 percent of their total traffic fatalities.
- More 18-year-olds died in lower BAC (between .01 and .09) alcohol-related crashes than any other age. In fact, 17-, 18-, 19-, 20-, 21- and 22-year olds are the top 6 ages of people that die in low BAC crashes.

More Young People Die in Crashes

- Youth are still over represented in fatal crashes compared to the older population. The rate of involvement is greater for youth for both alcohol- and non-alcohol-related crashes based on the total population, on the licensed driver population and on miles driven.
- Over 58 percent of the people that died in crashes where a young driver was involved were young people themselves. 8,807 people of all ages died in these crashes. 3,661 people who were not ages 15 through 20 died in these crashes.

- Three-quarters of the people who died in crashes where a young driver was drinking were young people themselves.
- In 1998, more 18-year-olds died in motor vehicle crashes than any other single age (1,395 fatalities). More 21-year-olds died in alcohol-related crashes than any other age (641).
- The six years of age from 15 through 20 account for over one-fifth of all passenger fatalities (21.7%).

Who and Where

- The greatest number of youth fatalities occur in June, July and August. The fewest occur in January through April.
- Approximately twice as many young people die in weekend crashes, per day, as on weekdays. Approximately three times as many young people die in alcohol-related crashes, per day, on weekends than on weekdays.
- Almost two-thirds of youth motor vehicle fatalities occurred in rural areas.
- In 1998, the State of New York had the lowest youth alcohol-related fatality rate at 3.8 fatalities per 100,000 population, followed by Utah at 3.9. No other state had a fatality rate less than 5. The national rate was 9.5.
- In 1998, Utah had the lowest percentage of crash fatalities that were alcohol-related for youth (14.9%). South Carolina had the second lowest percentage (16.5%). The National percentage was 35.8%.

New Laws Prevent Fatalities

- In 1998, about 7 percent of licensed drivers were ages 15 through 20. However, approximately 14 percent of drivers involved in fatal crashes were in this age group.
- The proportions of young fatally injured drivers and young drivers involved in fatal crashes who were intoxicated (BAC of .10 or above) have decreased significantly since 1982. The reduction in the number of drivers who were intoxicated dropped by almost 65 percent in both categories—the largest decline of any age group.
- The number of young people who died in a crash where an intoxicated young driver was involved declined by over 63% since 1982, from 2,763 to 1,011.
- Per mile driven, 16-year-old drivers have the highest rate of fatal crash involvement by a wide margin.
- For every 100,000 licensed drivers, young drinking drivers are involved in fatal crashes at approximately twice the rate of drivers aged 21 and older.
- NHTSA estimates that minimum drinking age laws have saved 18,220 lives since 1975. In 1998 alone, these laws saved 861 lives. All states and the District of Columbia have 21-year-old minimum drinking age laws. (Note: These are lives saved of all ages involving 18- to 20-year-old drivers in fatal crashes.)
- As of June 1998, all States and the District of Columbia have set a BAC limit of .02 or lower for drivers under the age of 21 (Zero Tolerance Laws).

- Twenty-three states now require (as of November 1, 1999) their young novice drivers to pass through a Graduated Driver Licensing (GDL) system. Graduated Driver Licensing is a three step licensing process that gradually phases in the licensing privilege as new skills are learned. These systems may include such features as: night time driving restrictions; certified hours of parental instruction; zero tolerance for alcohol and drugs; passenger restrictions; and accelerated sanctions for traffic violations. Some states do not provide for a full three-step licensing process, but include some individual component parts of the Graduated Driver Licensing system.

Underage Drinking Can Lead to Irresponsible Sexual Behavior

by Susan E. Foster

About the author: *Susan E. Foster is vice president and director of policy research and analysis at The National Center on Addiction and Substance Abuse at Columbia University.*

A recent PBS "Frontline" documentary chronicled an outbreak of syphilis among a large circle of teens in a suburban Atlanta community. What was even more alarming to health officials and the community was the revelation of a pattern of sex among upwards of 200 teens, focused around a group of girls, some as young as 13, with multiple partners, drinking and drug use, little if any protection, with no regard for the consequences.

Disturbing Connection

The events in Georgia raise the question of whether this was an isolated incident or a harbinger of teen life around the country. What is certain is the disturbing connection between teen drinking and drug use and the increased likelihood of sexual activity.

A new report released by The National Center on Addiction and Substance Abuse at Columbia University (CASA) raises troubling concerns about substance use and teen sexual activity: Teens who drink or use drugs are much more likely to have sex, initiate it at younger ages and have multiple partners, placing them at higher risk for sexually transmitted diseases (STDs), AIDS and unplanned pregnancies.

The report, "Dangerous Liaisons: Substance Abuse and Sex," is the result of a two-year, unprecedented analysis of the connection between drinking, drug use and sexual activity. The report's sobering conclusion finds that in America, drinking and drug abuse are bundled with high-risk sex.

Reprinted, by permission of the author, from "Teen-agers and Temptation: Early Use of Booze, Drugs, Leads to Sex and Problems," *The San Diego Union-Tribune*, January 23, 2000.

Before graduating high school, and even as early as middle school—among 10- to 13-years-olds—every teen will have to make a conscious choice whether to drink or use illegal drugs and whether to have sex. Many teens will be confronted with these decisions at the same time.

CASA's analysis shows that almost 80 percent of high school students have experimented with alcohol at least once. More than half had used at least one illicit drug. CASA's report noted the dramatic increase in just a generation of the proportion of 15-year-olds having sex: according to national surveys in 1970, less than 5 percent of 15-year-old girls and in 1972, 20 percent of 15-year-old boys, had engaged in sex. CASA's own analysis reveals that in 1997, 38 percent of 15-year-old girls and 45 percent of 15-year-old boys have had sex.

Among the report's key findings:

- Teens 14 and younger who use alcohol are twice as likely to have sex than those who don't.
- Teens 14 and younger who use drugs are four times likelier to have sex than those who don't.
- Teens 15 and older who drink are seven times likelier to have sexual intercourse and twice as likely to have it with four or more partners than nondrinking teens.
- Teens 15 and older who use drugs are five times likelier to have sexual intercourse and three times likelier to have it with four or more partners than those who don't.

Sixty-three percent of teens who use alcohol have had sex compared to 26 percent of those who never drank. Among teens who use drugs, 72 percent of teens have had sex compared to 36 percent who have never used drugs.

The Risk of Sexually Transmitted Diseases

Teens are more vulnerable to the combined lure of sex and alcohol and drugs. They are less able to cope with the potential consequences of drinking and using drugs which can undermine decisions about abstaining from sex, having unprotected sex and also trigger irresponsible and dangerous sexual behavior that can change the course of their lives.

The United States has the highest rate of STDs in the developed world. Teens are inconsistent condom users with or without alcohol and drugs which make the consequences of

> *"In America, drinking and drug abuse are bundled with high-risk sex."*

teen sexual activity linked to substance use clear: increased chances of infection by STDs such as syphilis, gonorrhea, chlamydia, as well as AIDS and unintended pregnancies.

While it is clear that teens who drink and use drugs are likelier to have sexual intercourse at earlier ages and with multiple partners, it is not clear which starts first—sexual intercourse or drinking or drug use. For parents, the point is that regardless of the sequence, either may be a red flag for the other. The report contains a loud and clear message for parents, clergy, school counselors and other caring adults: whichever teen activity—sex or substance use—first comes to their attention, these adults should be prepared to work with the teen on both matters.

The Power of Parents

Key to reducing a teen's risk of substance use is the power of parents. Parents have more influence over their children than they think. A CASA survey [*Back to School 1999—National Survey of American Attitudes on Substance Abuse V: Teens and Their Parents*] of 2,000 teens showed that 42 percent of teens who don't use marijuana credit their parents over any other influence; teens who used marijuana say their friends are the primary influence in their decision to try the drug.

The same CASA survey stressed the need for both parents to be engaged and involved in their children's lives. Many dads are AWOL in the battle to keep kids drug-free, increasing their teen's risk of substance abuse. The CASA survey found children living in two-parent families who have a fair or poor relationship with their father are at 68 percent higher risk of smoking, drinking and using drugs compared to the average teen. Teens consistently rate moms more favorably than dads: more teens report having a very good or excellent relationship with their moms, say it's easier to talk to mom about

"Teens are more vulnerable to the combined lure of sex and alcohol and drugs."

drugs, credit mom more with their decision not to use marijuana, and go to mom more often when they have important decisions to make. Mom also is more likely to monitor a teen's homework, grades or personal behavior more closely.

The safest teens are those living with two parents and who have a positive relationship with both. A teen living with a single mom who has an excellent relationship with that mother is also at lower risk than the average teen.

Sending the Right Message

CASA's earlier teen survey [*Back to School 1998—National Survey of American Attitudes on Substance Abuse IV: Teens, Teachers, and Principals*] also found that teens who attend a school where drugs are kept, used or sold are at twice the risk of substance abuse as teens attending a drug-free school. Schools can also do their part by creating comprehensive and age-appropriate education programs that address the association between substance abuse and sex.

When it comes to sex and substance abuse, how parents exercise their power in talking to their children about drinking, using drugs and engaging in sexual activity will be critical in how their children respond to the lure of alcohol, drugs and sex—as will the messages they send by their own behavior. For parents who believe that sexual abstinence before marriage is a moral imperative, the report signals the particular importance of persuading teens not to drink alcohol or use illegal drugs. For those parents who consider teen sexual activity an inevitable or appropriate rite of passage, the CASA report points up the greater dangers for those teens who do drink and use drugs.

Teen Alcohol Abuse May Cause Brain Damage

by Kathleen Fackelmann

About the author: *Kathleen Fackelmann writes on health issues for* USA Today *magazine.*

Teens who drink heavily face a slew of hazards, ranging from accidental injuries to death by alcohol poisoning. If early research is verified, scientists might add another danger to that list soon: brain damage.

Preliminary studies indicate that heavy, regular drinking can damage the developing brains of teens and young adults and perhaps destroy brain cells involved in learning and memory.

Recent scientific findings represent the first brush strokes of an emerging portrait of alcohol's impact on the young brain:

- Brain scans of teenagers who have abused alcohol suggest damage to the hippocampus, the region involved in learning and memory. On average, the young drinkers had a 10% smaller hippocampus than their peers, one study shows.
- A separate study shows that teens who are heavy drinkers perform poorly on memory tests.
- Brain scans of young women who drank heavily as teens showed regions of sluggish activity in the brain.

At risk: at least 3 million American teens who abuse alcohol regularly.

No Joke

People joke about the fact that alcohol kills brain cells, says Duncan Clark, a researcher at the University of Pittsburgh Medical Center. "Well, in this case, the implications are quite serious."

Clark and other scientists fear that teens and young adults who regularly get drunk will sustain lasting damage to the brain, which could make it more difficult for them to do well in school or at work.

Critics say it's too early to blame brain damage on alcohol abuse. They say that many teens who drink heavily also abuse other drugs and have other risk factors that could hurt the brain.

But researchers say that though the work is in the early stages, the evidence leans toward a link between alcohol and damage to young brains.

Surveys show that many young Americans favor the particularly dangerous binge drinking—downing four or five drinks in a row.

A recent survey by the Harvard School of Public Health in Boston found that 44% of college students are binge drinkers, and nearly 74% said they binged in high school.

"We have a massive alcohol problem among youth," says Enoch Gordis, the director of the National Institute on Alcohol Abuse and Alcoholism (NIAAA), a part of the National Institutes of Health in Bethesda, Md. Gordis and other experts say the new studies, although far from complete, represent a warning that alcohol may target the young brain. "Teens who drink heavily may not realize their maximum potential," Gordis says.

Until recently, researchers thought the teen brain had completed its development. Now scientists realize that the brain makes important strides until age 20 or 21.

Aaron White, a researcher at Duke University Medical Center in Durham, N.C., and his colleagues wondered whether that meant the young brain presented an especially vulnerable target for alcohol.

"Brain scans of teenagers who have abused alcohol suggest damage to the hippocampus."

The team injected young rats with a high dose of alcohol—the human equivalent of drinking a 12-pack in a single night. The rats got a day off, then got another shot the next day. The team continued that bingeing pattern for 20 days.

The team let the rats mature into adults, then challenged them with a memory maze. Initially, the rats did fine. But researcher H. Scott Swartzwelder wondered whether the rats had sustained a subtle brain injury, one that would show up under duress. To find out, the rats were given a single injection of alcohol and placed in the maze.

That slight impairment didn't mar the performance of rats that had never been given alcohol. Nor did it slow down rats that had been given alcohol as adults. But rats given shots of alcohol as adolescents faltered. Again and again, those rats made mistakes.

"'They were doing twice as bad as everyone else,'" Swartzwelder says.

Hippocampus May Be Hurt

The team thinks that the alcohol injured the hippocampus, a brain region involved in memory and learning. The findings are in the August 2000 issue of *Alcoholism: Clinical and Experimental Research*.

Other research suggests that binge drinking overloads a protein receptor on cells in the hippocampus, White says. When working properly, the receptors help the brain encode recent events. The proteins help lay down a memory so that it can be recalled.

Researchers think that binge drinking may lead to the death of cells in the hippocampus. The loss of those brain cells may underlie the rats' poor performance on the memory maze, Swartzwelder says.

There's also human research suggesting that teens and young adults who binge are hammering the hippocampus.

Adults who drink heavily for 20 or 30 years are known to damage that

"Teens who drink heavily may not realize their maximum potential."

brain region. But the injury was thought to be inflicted over decades of bathing the brain in toxic alcohol, says Michael De Bellis, a researcher at the University of Pittsburgh Medical Center. De Bellis and his colleagues recruited 12 teens and young adults with serious drinking problems. They took scans of their brains and compared them with those of 24 kids who did not have an alcohol problem.

On average, the drinkers had a 10% smaller hippocampus than their peers, a "substantial difference," co-author Clark says. The longer a youth had been drinking, the smaller the hippocampus.

The small study, which appears in the May 2000 issue of *The American Journal of Psychiatry,* does not prove that alcohol, rather than some other factor, damages the hippocampus, De Bellis cautions.

But those findings fit with another MRI study, this one of 10 young women who had abused alcohol as teens. All 10 had stopped drinking before the study.

The researchers used a type of MRI that snapped pictures of the brain while the women took a test—in this case, they had to remember the location of objects on a computer screen. Compared with 10 healthy young women, the women with a drinking history had trouble remembering the locations of objects, says Susan Tapert, a co-author who is at the University of California, San Diego.

The scans of the 10 former drinkers show sluggish brain regions. The worry is that alcohol damaged parts of the brain involved in spatial memory. In the real world, such damage could lead to trouble doing math or even reading a map, Tapert says.

And the study suggests that the brain damage, if it exists, is long-lasting. Some of the women in the study, who were in their late teens and early 20s, had been alcohol-free for months. Yet they still showed impairment in brain function, co-author Sandra Brown says.

Setting the Stage for Underachievement

The San Diego team has uncovered additional signs of thinking problems in a study of 33 teens, 15 and 16, who had been drinking heavily for several years.

The researchers gave the teens a list of names and 20 minutes later asked them to repeat it. The 24 members of the control group, who had no history of drinking, remembered 95% of the names. Those who had abused alcohol got 85%, Tapert says.

That's like getting a B instead of an A on a test, she says. The researchers described their results in the February 2000 issue of *Alcoholism: Clinical and Experimental Research*.

Again, the implication is that alcohol harmed regions of the brain involved in memory. The drinking teens had trouble remembering names—a problem that could translate to forgetting facts during a school test and might set the stage for spiraling underachievement, Brown says.

Those findings suggest that alcohol attacks the brain, although all three research teams say their results fall short of an indictment. It's almost impossible to find alcohol abusers who haven't used other drugs such as marijuana, they say. It could be marijuana, and not the alcohol, causing the memory difficulties, says Linda Spear, an alcohol and drug researcher at the State University of New York, Binghamton. And the MRI studies are far too small to offer any proof of brain damage, she says.

Don't Give Up on Youths

There has been a "'rush to judgment" on the part of the research community, Spear says.

She worries that people will write off young alcohol abusers as hopelessly damaged.

"'We have to be cautious," says Kenneth Sher, an alcohol researcher at the University of Missouri in Columbia. The studies to date have not conclusively proved that alcohol causes damage in the young brain. "'Yet the findings are extremely provocative," he says.

His research suggests that teens who drink heavily have trouble on cognitive tests. His findings suggest that the brain is most vulnerable to alcohol's toxic assault in the teen years, not during college.

"Even if research rules out brain damage, there is concern that heavy drinking can lead to short-term memory impairment."

Swartzwelder says he would bet on the theory that alcohol harms the brain throughout young adulthood. "The converging lines of evidence provide a very compelling argument," he says.

At the very least, the findings should raise a red flag for parents, teachers and others, Brown says. Kids with alcohol problems should get into treatment as quickly as possible, she says. If further research does prove brain damage from heavy drinking, the injury might be reversed, she says.

Even if research rules out brain damage, there is concern that heavy drinking can lead to short-term memory impairment, Swartzwelder says. Alcohol is thought to disrupt brain receptors that form memories, he says. So even if brain cells don't die, a heavy dose of alcohol will garble the ability to encode recent facts and events. Therefore, kids who study all day and drink at night might have trouble getting their facts right on a test the next day.

Swartzwelder has a simple message for students: "'Alcohol is bad for your memory.'"

Binge Drinking Can Cause Alcohol Poisoning

by Dixie M. Jordan

About the author: *Dixie M. Jordan is the publisher of parent-teen.com, an online magazine that focuses on delivering straightforward information to parents and teens.*

If you drink—or your friends do—here are things you need to know about alcohol poisoning.

So, what is alcohol poisoning?

It's not just having a hangover or drinking so much that you vomit. Alcohol poisoning happens when the blood alcohol level (the percentage of alcohol circulating in the bloodstream) rises to a danger point. At very high blood alcohol levels, a person loses consciousness and goes into a coma. In the worst cases, the drinker dies.

When you hear about someone dying from "alcohol poisoning," it usually means the person died in one of these three ways:

- The blood alcohol level was so high that it affected parts of the brain and nervous system that control breathing, heartbeat, and related body functions. The drinker died because he stopped breathing and his heart stopped beating, usually while unconscious.
- He vomited while unconscious, inhaled the vomitus, and suffocated. There are also occasional reports of an unconscious drinker choking on his own tongue.
- The alcohol reacted in combination with some other drug—over the counter, prescription, or illegal. These deaths can happen at a relatively low blood alcohol level.

An intoxicated person can also die of exposure, sometimes in temperatures as high as 50 degrees F. Alcohol affects both the body's "thermostat" and the drinker's perception of heat and cold; someone who's been drinking can feel warm while his body temperature is actually dropping.

If a Friend's Been Drinking

My friend drank a lot at a party and she's pretty drunk. She just wants to sleep it off. Is that okay?

Only if you are willing to stay with her, stay awake all night, and check on her continuously. When someone drinks a lot, or drinks rapidly, there can be a lag time before medical complications show up. Sleeping it off can progress into coma, and even death.

College health services advise taking these precautions:

- Make sure your friend doesn't have any cuts, scrapes or other injuries that need treatment.
- Turn her on her side in bed, and prop her up so that she cannot roll onto her back. This lessens the chances of choking if she vomits. Keep her warm. Give her water if she can drink it.
- Stay with her and check regularly for signs of alcohol poisoning.

What should I look for?

Bacchus and Gamma, a college peer alcohol education network, says the following symptoms are among those that signal a medical emergency. Call an ambulance if you see any one of the following:

- The person is unconscious and can't be awakened by pinching, prodding, or shouting.
- The skin is cold, clammy, pale, or bluish or purplish in color, all signs of insufficient oxygen.
- Slow or labored breathing, especially fewer than eight breaths a minute or more than ten seconds between breaths.
- Vomiting without waking up.

The Prevalence of Alcohol Poisoning

Isn't alcohol poisoning pretty rare?

Only a few cases of alcohol poisoning make national headlines—usually ones involving fraternity parties or initiations. But U.S. vital statistics show that more than 20,000 people a year die from alcohol induced causes. That figure does not include people killed in alcohol-related auto accidents or those who die of cirrhosis and other liver ailments.

> *"More than 20,000 people a year die from alcohol-induced causes."*

What drugs can cause bad reactions with alcohol?

Lots of legal and illegal drugs, from antidepressants to aspirin, can act in combination with alcohol.

Among the most dangerous are narcotic painkillers (including cough syrup with codeine, Tylenol® with codeine, Percodan®), and drugs classified as sedative-hypnotics (including barbiturates).

How many drinks does it take to cause alcohol poisoning?

It's not only how many drinks, but how quickly you drink them, how much you weigh, and whether you are male or female.

Other factors, including fatigue, how recently you've eaten, and a host of others can also affect individual reactions. And the faster you drink, the more quickly your blood alcohol level rises.

The liver metabolizes about a half ounce of pure alcohol per hour, the amount found in the "standard drink" usually used to calculate blood alcohol.

That's 1.25 oz of hard liquor (Scotch, vodka, rum, gin)—a single shot, not a double; or a 12-oz bottle of domestic beer; or 5.5 oz of table wine (about two-thirds of a cup). Each of these contains about the same amount of ethanol, the kind of alcohol that's found in liquor.

Although people think they "don't get as drunk" on beer or wine as on hard liquor, each of these drinks has the same physiological effect on the body.

The "one drink per hour" rule of thumb won't necessarily keep you below the legal definition of intoxication (in many states, .08 percent blood alcohol level, or BAL), but potentially fatal alcohol poisoning generally occurs at substantially higher levels than this.

Alcohol poisoning most often occurs when someone drinks relatively rapidly, often because of a drinking game, drinking contest, 21 shots for a 21st birthday celebration, "forced" drinking of large quantities (at a fraternity initiation, for instance), or "drinking to get drunk."

A woman weighing around 100 pounds can easily reach danger level with maybe half a dozen drinks in an hour, seven or eight over the course of two hours, and considerably less if she's taken a medication that reacts with alcohol.

Binge Drinking Can Cause a Variety of Problems

by Kathiann M. Kowalski

About the author: *Kathiann M. Kowalski is a health writer for various magazines.*

Twenty-year-old Benjamin was too young to drink legally, but that didn't keep him from "funneling" at an off-campus keg party with his fraternity brothers from Louisiana State University. Drinkers gulped down beer shots through a rubber hose into their mouths. Next, Benjamin and his group visited a bar near campus and chugged mixtures of rum, whiskey, and liqueur. By the end of the night, Benjamin had downed the equivalent of 24 drinks. With a blood alcohol level six times the adult legal limit, Benjamin died of acute alcohol poisoning.

On a Binge

A study by the Harvard School of Public Health found as many as 70 percent of students at some college campuses binge drink. One-third of all schools surveyed reported bingeing by more than half the students. The study defined binge drinking as five drinks in a row for men and four drinks in a row for women.

But the problem starts long before college. At least half of drinkers like Benjamin's fraternity brothers are already bingeing in high school. MADD—Mothers Against Drunk Driving—estimates half of America's 20 million junior and senior high school students drink monthly. Seventy-nine percent say being drunk feels good. Two-thirds or 66 percent say drinking helps them forget problems. A similar percentage admit they drink because others do it too.

In an informal survey of 30 high school sophomores by 15-year-old John Morth of Cleveland Heights, Ohio, 56 percent admitted they had gotten drunk through unsupervised use of alcohol. All but one student said it was "easy" or "very easy" to get alcohol. "What did surprise me was how young kids were when they started using alcohol," says John. In his survey, the average age when students first used alcohol was 12; this is the same as the national average for all teens.

Reprinted from "The Dangers of Alcohol," by Kathiann M. Kowalski, *Current Health 2*, February 1998, by permission of Weekly Reader Corporation.

Living with a Binge Drinker

Binge drinkers affect the lives of other people—not just their own. Eighteen-year-old Nicole hadn't been at college a full week before her freshman roommate stored two cases of beer under the bed in violation of campus rules. That first semester, Nicole's roommate came in drunk nearly every night, sometimes bringing other people back with her. "Living with a binge drinker disrupted my sleep habits, my study habits, and my emotional well-being," Nicole says. "After a while, I was at the point where I was only getting three hours of sleep each night."

Nicole couldn't study in her room, and study groups and friends stayed away too. "I often felt very lonely as a result," recalls Nicole, who is now a junior. "I had gone from being an honor student surrounded by friends to someone who was struggling to study and felt completely alone."

Although Nicole complained, the small private college she attended in Ohio didn't let her change rooms until mid-February.

Unfortunately, sometimes it takes a tragedy to bring about a response. For some time, there were noted alcohol abuse problems at Massachusetts Institute of Technology (MIT). Yet it wasn't until the fall of 1997, when an 18-year-old freshman died amid vomit and liquor bottles, that MIT took significant steps to curb underage drinking.

What Alcohol Does to Our Body

When a person takes a drink of alcohol, ethanol (the chemical name for drinkable alcohol) irritates the stomach lining, releasing acids. A small amount is broken down chemically, but most of the alcohol heads toward the small intestine through an opening called the pyloric valve. Drinking too much alcohol too quickly can cause the valve to swell and close, causing vomiting.

From the small intestine, alcohol speeds into the bloodstream and toward the brain, where it depresses the central nervous system. By affecting the brain's production of chemicals called neurotransmitters, alcohol alters the person's behavior and the body's ability to function. Brain functions slow, decreasing balance, eyesight, and reasoning ability.

A "drink" is 12 ounces of beer or wine cooler, 4 ounces of wine, or 1 ounce of 86-proof whiskey. With one drink, a 160-pound adult male's

"Drinkers can—and do—get into violent fights."

blood alcohol level rises to 0.02 (2/10 of a gram of alcohol per 100 milliliters of blood). The drinker may feel relaxed and carefree.

Two and a half drinks in an hour shoots our 160-pound male's blood alcohol level up to 0.05. (The level is even higher for women, because they absorb more alcohol per drink into the bloodstream than men due to different enzyme levels in the stomach.) The drinker feels "high," and judgment is clearly affected. With alcohol blocking brain functions that restrain certain behaviors, the drinker may get loud and rowdy.

Shouting insults and taking offense at comments that normally would be shrugged off, drinkers can—and do—get into violent fights. Other drinkers wind up in riots like those that erupted in September 1997 at the University of New Hampshire. Teens who would never otherwise break the law could find themselves jailed for joy riding in a stolen car, holding up a liquor store, or other crimes. Young people who typically act responsible sexually may expose themselves to unwanted pregnancies or even AIDS by engaging in unprotected intercourse.

At about 0.10 blood alcohol level, the drinker loses practically all judgment, dexterity, and coordination. Slurring words and staggering around the room, drinkers insist they are not drunk. At a blood alcohol level of 0.20, the drinker may explode in a violent rage, yet not even remember it later. Between 0.40 and 0.50, the person sinks into a coma.

When drinkers use other drugs, too, they run even more serious health risks. Consuming alcohol and depressant pills, for example, multiplies the effects—and the dangers—of each drug.

It Takes Time to Sober Up

Like sand flowing constantly through an hour glass, alcohol flows through the body until it is metabolized, or chemically broken down. No amount of coffee, exercise, or "chasers" can speed the process.

"First-pass metabolism" of part of the alcohol occurs in the stomach, and about 5 percent of the alcohol is released unchanged through sweat and breath. The greater portion of the alcohol, however, must be processed by the liver. Acetaldehyde dehydrogenase (ADH) converts ethanol to acetaldehyde. Acetaldehyde is further converted to acetic acid and then to carbon dioxide and water. The process takes about an hour per drink in a 160-pound adult male.

"Teens can ruin their lives through chronic drinking."

While this occurs, the liver can't function effectively in its normal job of converting stored fats and other nutrients into glucose, the sugar used by the body for energy. Over time, heavy drinkers can develop fatty deposits in the liver or suffer cirrhosis, a fatal disease involving scarring and hardening of the liver tissue.

Even after alcohol is metabolized, the body needs time to recover from the drug's onslaught. An all-too-common result is a hangover: throbbing headache, dull eyes, grogginess, and dehydration.

A Slow Poison

Even if drinking doesn't lead to acute alcohol poisoning, teens can ruin their lives through chronic drinking. Over time, the body builds up a resistance to alcohol, craving more of the drug to get the same "high." Teens are more susceptible to developing addictions because they are still growing, both physically and emotionally. Approximately 3.3 million Americans ages 12 to 26 are problem drinkers.

Alcohol addiction can be devastating. A dramatic drop in grades and increased absenteeism can be the least of a young alcoholic's problems. Drunkenness can lead to violence, and other crimes, such as stealing and robbery, to pay for more alcohol.

> *"Alcoholism can be treated, but there is no miracle cure."*

Personal relationships dissolve into nothing. Tensions between teens and parents can go from bad to worse. Friendships disappear, until the only people around are those who also drink or use drugs.

Over time, alcohol wears away the body. If acute alcohol poisoning, violence, or an accident doesn't kill a chronic drinker, chances are increased risks of liver disease, heart disease, and cancer will.

One-for-the-Road Can Kill

Seventeen-year-old Brandon propped a beer between his legs as he drove through Gulfport, Mississippi, on Super Bowl Sunday in 1995. Two more beers sat on the front seat. Not realizing that traffic had stopped, Brandon slammed his pickup truck into the car in front of him, crushing 4-year-old Whitney in the back seat. After 49 hours in a coma, Whitney died. Convicted in Mississippi's Harrison County Circuit Court of "driving under the influence causing death," Brandon was sentenced to 20 years in prison. He must pay a nominal amount each week to Whitney's parents, but nothing can ever bring their child back.

Brandon's story is not unique. In 1995, 1.4 million people were arrested for driving while intoxicated, subjecting them to license suspension, criminal conviction, and jail time. In 1997, 19-year-old Oksana Baiul was arrested when she crashed her Mercedes at 2:30 a.m. on an icy road in Connecticut. Suffering a concussion and scalp wound, the Olympic gold medalist had a blood alcohol level of 0.168.

According to the National Highway Traffic Safety Administration, alcohol-related crashes killed 17,126 people in the U.S. in 1996. While this was a 1 percent overall decrease from 1995 figures, SADD—Students Against Destructive Decisions—reports that alcohol-related motor vehicle deaths for young people ages 15 to 20 increased 5 percent to 2,315.

A federal law requires that all states have a zero tolerance law for drivers under age 21 by the end of 1998. This means that if any alcohol is detected through breathalyzer or equivalent tests, teen drivers can be convicted.

What should you do if the driver for your ride home has been drinking? Even one drink can decrease the concentration and coordination needed to drive safely. Try to persuade the driver to hand over the keys. Do whatever you can to prevent the person from driving. But if you can't, don't get into the car! Call a parent to pick you up, or take a cab home.

Getting Help

Alcohol abusers find every creative way to deny they have a problem: They don't drink as much as other people do. They can "hold their liquor." They're "in control."

But tough questions like these can reveal the truth:

- Do you feel uncomfortable when alcohol isn't available?
- Do you ever miss school, work, or social activities because of alcohol?
- Do you spend a lot of time hungover?
- Do you drink more than usual when you're under pressure?
- Do you binge drink?
- Do you ever feel guilty about drinking?
- Do you resent when people talk about your drinking?
- Have you ever been unable to remember parts of the evening before?

Answering "yes" to any of these questions probably means you need help.

Fortunately, lots of sources offer help. Doctors, guidance counselors, or health departments can recommend medical help to cope with the physical effects of withdrawal, or detoxification. They also can refer teens to professionals who can address social and psychological problems related to drinking.

Alcoholics Anonymous offers free help for staying sober, one day at a time. Recovering alcoholics who understand the difficulties of the disease provide guidance and support for new members. In addition to regular meetings, many chapters offer meetings and conferences just for young people. A related organization, Alateen, offers support to teens who have alcoholic friends and family members, even if the alcoholic won't yet admit to a drinking problem.

Alcoholism can be treated, but there is no miracle cure. Instead, a person must work each day to stay sober. It's a tough job, with setbacks along the way. But the gains in good health are immeasurable.

Chapter 3

Does Alcohol Advertising Encourage Teens to Drink?

Chapter Preface

The debate over whether beer, wine, and liquor companies should be allowed to advertise their products on television has gained national prominence because of two key developments. First, in the so-called "tobacco wars" of the 1990s, the American public learned, from tobacco industry documents that were made public, that for decades the major tobacco companies had been subtly marketing cigarettes to young people. Many public health advocates began questioning whether the alcohol industry has also targeted young people with its advertising. Second, in June 1996 the Seagram Company began airing ads for its Crown Royal Canadian whiskey on television, thus ending a voluntary fifty-year ban on the airing of liquor ads on television. The move led many parents and politicians to question whether alcohol advertisements should be allowed on television.

Critics argue that alcohol ads that feature animals, such as the Budweiser frogs, or that show young (albeit not underage) people at parties have inherent youth appeal. William Beaver, a professor of social science at Robert Morris College, summarizes the concern over the influence of alcohol advertising on youth: "Children exposed to alcohol advertising over a period of years can gain a false impression about drinking (it's always good!), which becomes part of their value system and influences later drinking behavior." James F. Mosher, a senior policy adviser at the Marin Institute for the Prevention of Alcohol and Other Drug Problems, charges that this is the intended goal of alcohol advertising: "As with tobacco, beer marketers target teen-agers. They know that the earlier you start to drink the more likely you are to become a heavy drinker."

Industry spokesmen have vehemently denied any link between advertising and underage drinking. Jeffrey Becker, a vice president of the Beer Institute, an industry trade group, says "there's not a single credible study that shows advertising encourages young people to drink." "The beer industry markets to people legally able to buy the product," he insists. The best way to prevent underage drinking, according to the alcohol industry, is to enforce the laws that bar sales of alcohol to those under twenty-one. Anheuser-Busch vice president Francine Katz says teens who drink should not be seen as "hapless victims" of advertising: "The fact that they may like a commercial is no excuse to break the law. There isn't a young person in America who doesn't know it's illegal to drink."

The authors in the following chapter further explore this debate over whether alcohol advertising encourages teens to drink.

Alcohol Advertising Encourages Teens to Drink

by Mediascope

About the author: *Mediascope is a national, nonprofit research and policy organization working to promote issues of social relevance within the entertainment industry.*

During January 1995, three animated Budweiser frogs were introduced on television, croaking in sequence the words *"Bud," "wei"* and *"ser."* One year later, children aged 9 to 11 years were almost as familiar with the Budweiser frogs as they were with Bugs Bunny, and more familiar with what the three frogs croaked than they were with Smokey the Bear, the Mighty Morphin' Power Rangers and Kellogg's Frosted Flakes' Tony the Tiger. Budweiser advertising, along with other beer advertising campaigns, have made these young children aware of beer, even though they may not be legally allowed to purchase alcohol for another decade.

Alcohol Advertisements Glamorize Drinking

Children's television viewing habits leave them widely exposed to pervasive, attractive promotions for alcohol. Before reaching the legal drinking age, young people view thousands of alcohol advertisements on television. Characteristics such as animation, humor and rock music are attracting young people, especially children aged 10 to 14 years, to alcohol advertisements. Beer advertisements often glamorize drinking and provide no information about the potential negative effects alcohol has on the body, including nausea, blackouts and liver problems.

Advocates are pointing to a recent study of the effects of alcohol on youth that showed 470 students (seventh to tenth grade) advertisements for beer, wine and soda. It concluded that youth who said they paid more attention to alcohol commercials were more likely to report that they consumed alcoholic beverages. Related to this conclusion, a recent study performed by the Center for Science in the Public Interest and the Children of Alcoholics revealed that beer advertisements are teaching American youth that it is safe to drink alcohol.

Reprinted from "Youth-Oriented Alcohol Advertising," by Mediascope, *Issue Briefs*, March 9, 2000, published at www.mediascope.org/pubs/ibriefs/yoaa.htm. Reprinted by permission of Mediascope Press.

Underage drinking remains a widespread problem. Young people are beginning to consume alcohol around the age of 13. A large majority will do their heaviest drinking before their 21st birthday. A 1995 Monitoring the Future Study revealed that high school seniors use alcohol as their main substance of choice (64%); in comparison with 42% smoking cigarettes; 32% using marijuana; and 6% using cocaine.

For the past fifty years, liquor companies have voluntarily agreed not to air their advertisements in broadcast media. In the summer of 1996, however, Seagram Co. decided to disregard the voluntary ban on television and radio advertisements for hard liquor and aired their commercials for Seagram's Crown Royal Canadian whisky on a Texas station. The rest of the industry followed Seagram's lead. Despite protests from alcohol-control activists, the Distilled Spirits Council of the United States decided to end the fifty year ban because of lagging liquor sales in favor of the wine and beer industry. The major broadcast networks have said they do not plan to change their policy against accepting liquor advertisements, but some cable networks, such as BET (Black Entertainment Television) and Continental Cablevision Inc. have decided to run the hard liquor commercials.

Beer and wine marketers never voluntarily abstained from airing their commercials on the television or radio stations. Brewers spend more than $600 million a year on television and radio advertising, which does not include the $90 million spent on print advertisements. Liquor companies currently spend about $90 million in print advertising, but with some companies disregarding the broadcast ban, advertising dollars could potentially escalate.

Recently, the Federal Trade Commission (FTC) began investigating television commercials placed by Stroh Brewery Co. and Seagram Co. The investigation entails determining the number of viewers under 21 watching alcohol commercials. In addition, if there is a significant number of younger viewers, the FTC will look at the advertisement's content, scheduled time slots, and demographic information. [Editor's note: The FTC report, issued in September 1999, calls on the alcohol industry to institute self-regulatory advertising codes.]

Strategies to Combat Alcohol Advertising

Despite studies that indicate alcohol use is dangerous for young people, most youth are naming alcohol as their number one drug of choice. Some experts have called for a combination of public policy, education, parental guidance and community strategies to be implemented to combat children's fascination with alcohol and alcohol-related advertising. Public health experts cite a variety of strategies that can be implemented. These include:

- Restricting television alcohol advertising during prime viewing hours for children, such as on weekend mornings, early prime-time and during sports programs, and limiting alcohol sponsorship of sports and other events that youth might attend.

- Promoting cooperation between alcohol advertising and alcohol prevention advocates to reduce the extent to which alcohol advertising or promotion appeals to young people. For example, researchers could provide feedback concerning the types of commercials that are appealing to children and offer suggestions for improving the advertisements.
- Counteradvertising or public service messages warning youth about the dangers of alcohol.
- Helping young people develop media literacy skills in school so they have the ability to recognize and understand the persuasive appeal of advertising.

Liquor Advertisements Should Not Be Televised

by Bill Clinton

About the author: *Former president Bill Clinton issued the following remarks in response to the 1996 decision by several liquor companies to begin showing liquor advertisements on television.*

The Vice President and I have worked very hard . . . to help parents protect the health and the safety of their children. Our parents face enormous pressures today, greater than ever before, and they need our help as they try to guard their children from harmful influences.

That's why we fought to impose appropriate regulation on the sale and distribution of cigarettes and smokeless tobacco and on the advertising of these products in a way that appeals to young people, why we're working to make our schools and children safe and drug-free, to combat gangs and youth violence.

It's a fact that popular culture is not always popular with parents, because it's not always good for their children. That was the thinking behind the V-chip and the television rating systems, which together will help parents to better control which programs their children watch. You need only to turn on the television for an evening to know there are some things that children should not be watching.

The Responsible Thing to Do

We're here today because parents now face a new challenge in protecting their children, the advertising of liquor on television. For half a century, for as long as television has been around, this has not been an issue. The distilled spirit industry voluntarily did not advertise on television. The reason was simple: It was the responsible thing to do. Liquor has no business with kids, and kids should have no business with liquor. Liquor ads on television would provide a message of encouragement to drink that young people simply don't need. Nothing good can come of it.

Today our message to the liquor industry is simple: For 50 years you have kept the ban; it is the responsible thing to do. For the sake of our parents and

Reprinted from "Remarks on the Advertising of Distilled Liquor and an Exchange with Reporters," by Bill Clinton, in *Weekly Compilation of Presidential Documents*, April 7, 1997.

our young people, please continue to keep that ban.

I want to thank the television networks and the many television stations all across America which have shunned these new liquor ads. They have acted responsibly. I urge them to remain steadfast. I also want to thank Reed Hundt, the Chairman of our Federal Communications Commission. He has spoken out strongly and plainly to broadcasters to keep the voluntary ban on TV advertising.

I agree with Chairman Hundt that the FCC has an obligation to consider any and all actions that would protect the public interest in the use of the public airwaves. So today I urge the FCC to take the next step. I want the Commission to explore the effects on children of the hard liquor industry's decision to advertise on television. And I want the FCC to determine what action is appropriate in response to that decision. [Editor's note: The FCC declined to launch an inquiry into the liquor industry's advertising practices.]

> *"Liquor ads on television would provide a message of encouragement to drink that young people simply don't need."*

Let me say directly again to the makers of distilled spirits: It should not require a Federal action to encourage you to continue to act responsibly. I have asked that liquor ads be kept off the air for the same reasons you yourself have kept them off the air for 50 long years. We must do nothing—nothing—that would risk encouraging more of our young people to drink hard liquor. That is simply common sense. Alcohol is a drug most abused by adolescents and teenagers. Studies show a strong connection between underage drinking and youth crime, including murder and rape. Year after year, underage drinking causes thousands of deadly car crashes.

As a nation, we've worked to bring down those numbers by increasing the drinking age to 21 and passing and enforcing zero-tolerance legislation for underage drinking and driving. We've taken that further. I've asked the Transportation Secretary, Rodney Slater and our drug czar, General McCaffrey, to develop an initiative to further reduce drug use and drunk driving by young people.

All these actions are aimed at helping parents to protect their children better and to help young people deal better with the temptation of bad influences. Now I think we should move urgently to save parents, young people, and our Nation from the unavoidable bad consequences of liquor advertising on television. I urge the manufacturers again to rethink their decision to break from their tradition of being responsible on this front. If they remain responsible, it will be easier for our young people to do so, and parents will have one less thing to worry about.

Barring that, we will work to find ways to respond to the decision by the distilled spirits industry. We will do what we must do to support our parents to help them do their jobs.

We dare not do anything less. . . .

No Backsliding

Reporter: *Mr. President, the industry is saying, why not beer and wine, also?*

The President: Well, for one thing, let's just focus on where we are now. The FCC is going to look at this whole issue, if they respond positively to my suggestion. But at a minimum, there should be no backsliding. Look at the evidence. If the evidence is as I suspect it will be, that a great deal of problem is caused by hard liquor ingestion already among young people and that advertising would cause it to be worse, then I think the FCC has grounds to act. But I think we ought to start with the principle of no backsliding. Let's don't make it worse.

> *"We must do nothing—nothing—that would risk encouraging more of our young people to drink hard liquor."*

Sir, the industry, in a sense, considers this a solution in search of a problem, because they have done so very little advertising on television at this point. How would you respond to that?

That's right, they have. And that's what we're trying to do, we're trying to nip it in the bud. We're trying to make it a dog that does not bark, if you will. It's not a solution in search of a problem; there was no problem before the announced intention to abandon the 50-year ban. And what we're trying to do is to nip it in the bud, hopefully and most importantly, by persuading them to stay with their policy.

This is an area where—you know, the liquor industry has really been remarkably responsible for five long decades when it would have been easy for financial reasons for them to try to take another course. And I understand the financial pressures they're under, but I hope that they will agree to go back and embrace their original position. If they don't, I think it's only responsible for the Federal Communications Commission to explore what the likely impact of this is and if it is appropriate for the FCC to take action. . . .

Alcohol is alcohol. If it sends a bad message to put ads on television that kids will see urging them to drink Seagrams, why wouldn't it send just as bad a message—the ads that they're seeing to urge them to drink Coors Lite or—

Well, again I will say, first of all, let's—there's something to be said for not making matters worse. And most of us, every day, make decisions in an imperfect environment in which we make responsible decisions. This is one thing adults have to do for their children all the time, in which you say, "Well, I'm not going to make a perfect decision here, but at least we're not going to make things worse." And that's the position we have taken.

I think the liquor industry itself once thought that there was a distinction to be drawn if, for no other reason than alcohol content, between beer and wine and hard liquor, which is why they observed this distinction for 50 years. They thought there was a distinction for 50 years; otherwise, they would not have observed it. That was their opinion for 50 years, and I think they were right. And so I would say, the FCC—if there is no difference, if there are problems—the FCC can evaluate whatever evidence comes in, and the liquor industry would be free to present that information to the FCC.

But I believe there is a distinction, and I think there is a very powerful argument for doing no harm. Why make things worse? Why backslide?

The Alcohol Industry Intentionally Markets Its Products to Youths

by David Walsh

About the author: *Psychologist David Walsh is founder and president of the National Institute on Media and the Family, an organization that works to help parents and other adults make informed choices by providing information about media products that are likely to impact on children.*

[In 1996] Seagrams broke a 60-year voluntary ban on liquor advertising on radio and television, an act that was greeted with an avalanche of negative reactions from children's advocates, health care people and political leaders of both parties. Nevertheless, liquor marketers are vowing to press on with plans to advertise over the airwaves.

[In July 1997] the Federal Communications Commission met to consider whether to launch an inquiry into regulating this potential advertising windfall for broadcasters. However, a 2-2 split blocked the attempt, which requires three votes. The five-member commission [had] one vacancy.

The two commissioners voting against the inquiry did so on the grounds that the matter of liquor advertising should be handled by the Federal Trade Commission, but one said he could reverse his course if the FTC fails to take appropriate action.

Should the FCC get involved? Is there reason to be concerned about liquor advertising and children? The answer to these questions is a resounding yes.

Problems Related to Underage Drinking

Every day there is a new report about the worrisome state of America's children. Statistics that show the highest rate of teenage pregnancy in the industrialized world and a tide of violence engulfing more and more young people top

Reprinted from "Kids and Liquor Ads," by David Walsh, *Washington Post*, July 11, 1997. Reprinted by permission of the author.

the list. While no one can blame the growing list of woes solely on alcohol, we know it is involved in many of our concerns about kids.

One study of adolescents with unplanned pregnancies found that almost 50 percent had been drinking and/or using drugs before the act of intercourse that resulted in the pregnancy. And in-depth analysis of youth homicides completed last year showed that nearly 60 percent of young victims had some level of alcohol in their blood at the time of death, with 33 percent being legally intoxicated. Alcohol is the cause of 50 percent of vehicle-related injuries and deaths among young drivers. Still other studies show alcohol is involved in most date rapes.

With statistics such as these, no one can argue that alcohol and kids mix. That's why every state has laws about underage drinking. But what does this have to do with the liquor industry decision? The answer is simple. We know radio and television advertising of alcohol encourages use among kids. We also know it works. We know this because we've been running an experiment for years. For while advertising of distilled spirits has not been on the airwaves, beer commercials have been. And the kids love them.

Advertisers Target Youth

A 1994 study of fifth- and sixth-graders showed that TV beer advertising was related to positive feelings about drinking and to an intention to drink. Eighty-eight percent of 12-year-olds could identify Spuds Mackenzie with Budweiser Beer. A report published in the *American Journal of Public Health* concludes that most available research on alcohol advertising and youth has shown a positive correlation between exposure to commercials and drinking behavior. One of the studies found that after viewing ads for beer, youth were more likely to drink, drink heavily and drink in hazardous situations. A survey conducted by the alcohol industry itself found that 73 percent of the public thought alcohol advertising is a major contributor to underage drinking.

None of this should come as a surprise when we consider two important factors. The first is that television and radio are the most popular media with kids. America's children spend more time watching TV than on any other activity of their waking lives. As children become teenagers, radio assumes a bigger and bigger role.

Second, alcohol advertisers, in spite of what they say, have to target youth. As any advertiser knows, a major goal is to establish brand loyalty before your competitors do. By creating loyal customers out of kids, advertising produces two benefits: defeating the competition and producing more years of return for the advertising investment.

"Beer commercials overwhelmingly link drinking with activities very popular with kids."

Consequently, there is no mystery involved when we realize that beer commercials are very youth-oriented. Beer commercials overwhelmingly link drinking with activities very popular with kids—volleyball, skiing, dancing, partying, etc. They also connect drinking with the emotional "hot buttons" for kids—popularity, sociability, physical attractiveness, adventure and romance. Not surprisingly, in a recent survey 16-year-olds listed beer commercials among their favorites. Compounding the concerns, 33 percent of TV beer commercials portray the alcohol use in potentially dangerous situations such as water sports or driving.

Beer advertising is especially high during televised sporting events. This creates the psychological connection that athletes and alcohol go together. High school athletes in most states, however, are barred from competition if they act on that suggestion. College administrators privately worry that beer companies are such prominent financial sponsors of campus activities in spite of the fact that most college students are too young to drink legally.

Protecting Children

So is there reason for us to be concerned about the liquor industry plan to advertise on radio and television? Absolutely. Should the FCC call for an inquiry? Yes.

The Federal Communications Commission is charged with safeguarding the interests of the public in the use of the airwaves. What could be a more important issue for the common good than protecting children from harm? To allow a 60-year ban to disappear without so much as an inquiry is not good policy. Not if we're serious about wanting the best for our children.

The Government Should Counter-Advertise to Combat the Influence of Alcohol Advertising

by George A. Hacker

About the author: *George A. Hacker directs the alcohol policies project at the Center for Science in the Public Interest, a nonprofit organization that promotes alcohol abuse prevention policies.*

After more than 50 years of honoring its pledge not to advertise distilled spirits in the broadcast media, the liquor industry lost its grip on good corporate citizenship in November 1996 and abandoned the voluntary ban.

As recently as 1993, the president of the Distilled Spirits Council of the United States (DISCUS) had described the ban to a Senate committee as part of the liquor industry's "responsibility to combat alcohol abuse." Now DISCUS has begun passing off liquor ads as consumer education. [In 1998] it ran a TV ad in the Washington, DC, market promoting both the alcohol equivalence of typical servings of beer, wine, and distilled spirits and the availability and fun of drinking spirits. Soon DISCUS will launch a multimillion-dollar ad campaign designed to put even more of a shine on liquor's tarnished image.

The decision to dump the restraint resulted from desperation over two decades of plummeting liquor consumption. Distillers envy the ability of beer marketers to use radio and television to reach mass audiences of young, heavy-drinking consumers. They lament having been the victims of their own and their regulators' restraints. In short, the industry suffers from a big inferiority complex that it now wants to cure. It is demanding equity, and, from the looks of its efforts thus far, it doesn't much matter to liquor producers whether equity comes in the form of more liquor ads on television or fewer, more restricted beer ads.

Reprinted from "Prevention and Liquor Commercials," by George A. Hacker, *Counselor*, January/February 1999. Reprinted with permission from the National Association of Alcoholism and Drug Abuse Counselors (NAADAC) www.naadac.org.

Do we really want to open the airwaves to liquor? For too long we have tolerated beer commercials that seduce young people into believing that drinking is the ticket to friendship, athletic prowess, sexual fulfillment, and happiness. In 1997, the airwaves carried some $720 million in beer and wine advertisements and just over $10 million in advertisements for distilled spirits.

Alcohol Ads and Teenagers

Note the results of this level of exposure: Junior high school students can name more beer brands than presidents. Budweiser ads are the most popular of all on television for children ages 7 through 16. More young children recognize the Budweiser frogs than all but one other commercial television critter. No wonder that beer is the alcoholic beverage of choice and a gateway drug for teenagers. Do we want young people to switch to liquor?

Television advertising of alcohol:

- affects the manner, style, and meaning of drinking in society
- defines beer drinking as a positive and normative behavior
- promotes an exaggerated view of how many people drink and how much
- provides drinking lessons for kids that ought to be left to parents and less self-interested parties

The liquor industry's call for equity and the experience so far with the few televised liquor advertisements leave little doubt that distillers want access to the same youthful targets so assiduously courted by the brewers. An expansion of broadcast liquor advertising could reach millions of underage persons who are not exposed to those messages now.

Drawing a line in the sand to block broadcast liquor advertising, as many advocacy groups have done, does not concede the legitimacy of beer and wine advertisements in broadcasting, nor does it accept the myth that beer and wine are somehow less harmful. It simply rejects backsliding and reflects a determination to protect children from additional, potentially harmful influences. Admittedly, it is a defensive effort rather than the solution to the problem of alcohol advertising.

Outside of the liquor and advertising industries and a few needy broadcasters, there is virtually no support for liquor advertisements on television. President Clinton and Senator Trent Lott (R-MS) agree that distillers should go back to the voluntary ban. Attorney General Janet Reno, like the

"Junior high school students can name more beer brands than presidents."

President and 26 members of Congress, has asked the Federal Communications Commission (FCC) to investigate what it can do to protect children from broadcast liquor advertisements. Fourteen state attorneys general went even further, petitioning the FCC to ban such advertisements.

Many proposals have been offered to combat the influence of broadcast liquor, beer and wine advertisements. None appears to be on a political fast track, but each presents lawmakers with potentially powerful tools to protect children and secure a better balance of societal information about America's most used and abused drug. The measures have broad popular support and the backing of the largest and most prestigious health, safety, religious, education, and anti-drug groups.

The proposed measures do not call for a blanket ban on broadcast alcohol advertising. They respect producers' right to convey truthful, non-misleading information about their products to adult consumers. They recognize the political and possible legal obstacles to formulating advertising standards that differentiate among beer, wine, and liquor. They are tailored narrowly to provide a balance of information helpful to consumers without impeding other avenues of commercial communications. Substantively and legally, they have ample precedent in the public health campaigns against tobacco, and they facilitate broadcasters' compliance with statutory obligations to operate in the public interest.

Mandatory Health and Safety Messages in Alcohol Ads

One measure that has been lurking in Congress since 1990 would require health and safety messages in all alcoholic-beverage advertising. The Sensible Advertising and Family Education Act, introduced by the just-retired Representative Joseph P. Kennedy II (D-MA), calls for a series of rotating warnings in advertisements. On television, the warnings would be displayed as banners during the advertisement, accompanied by a voiceover reading of the message. The messages would

> *"A mixture of commercials can provide effective relief from the one-sided promotion of drinking."*

caution consumers about alcohol risks, including underage drinking, drinking during pregnancy, drunk driving, drinking while taking certain medications, and drinking too much too fast.

Mandatory "counter ads" would help defuse the effects of alcohol ads. Such messages would provide information about the health and safety risks related to drinking and deglamorize over-consumption, drinking by underage persons, and alcohol consumption during pregnancy.

Experience with counter advertising during the "tobacco wars" and the Office of National Drug Control Policy's current federal anti-drug media campaign indicates that a mixture of commercials can provide effective relief from the one-sided promotion of drinking. In sufficient proportion to the commercials for alcoholic beverages and aired at times the target audience was viewing, counter ads, which eventually drove cigarette advertising from broadcast media, could have substantial informational and political impact. If produced by sources independent of the affected industries, mandatory counter ads might even be worth allowing liquor advertisements on the air.

Alcohol is not tobacco. Using our most powerful communications media to promote the use of liquor (and beer and wine) to substantial numbers of children, however, poses similar, serious public health and safety concerns. The liquor industry's new political and public relations strategies raise the visibility of those concerns. Big liquor may not get many advertisements on the air, but the attempt will help focus needed attention on the beer advertisements that drown our children today. Saying "no" to liquor advertisements is only a warm-up for saying "no" to those advertisements, too.

Alcohol Advertisements Should Be Restricted in Public Places

by Traci L. Toomey, Lara Pratt, Catherine Rothstein, Judy Meath, and Alexander Wagenaar

About the authors: *Traci L. Toomey, Lara Pratt, Catherine Rothstein, Judy Meath, and Alexander Wagenaar are researchers at the Alcohol Epidemiology Program, a project at the University of Minnesota School of Public Health that studies initiatives to prevent alcohol-related problems.*

Communities can restrict alcohol ads in public places to eliminate alcohol advertising where parents have limited control over young people's exposure to alcohol messages.

Restrictions on alcohol advertising can include:

* Banning ads from public places such as buses (inside and out), bus shelters, trains, kiosks, billboards, schools, supermarket carts, and theme parks;
* Restricting the size and placement of ads in the windows of alcohol establishments;
* Banning or limiting advertising and sponsorship at community events such as festivals, parties, rodeos, concerts, and sporting events;
* Starting a letter writing campaign to the Federal Government or to radio and television stations to ban or restrict commercials for alcohol on stations appealing to youth;
* Enforcing existing restrictions on alcohol advertising;
* Countering ads with public service announcements. Radio and television stations may be willing to donate time for health-related messages;
* Requiring all alcohol ads in the local media to include warnings about the health risks of alcohol consumption;
* Encouraging alcohol manufacturers and merchants to voluntarily restrict their alcohol advertising in the local newspaper, in store windows, etc.; and
* Restricting ads to a percentage of all advertising space in a municipality's

public spaces or in terms of their distance from schools, residential areas, churches, etc.

Why alcohol ad restrictions are important:

- Alcohol advertising often associates alcohol with economic success, fun, attractiveness to the opposite sex, athletic skill, and social popularity. Such messages are misleading to young people and fail to mention the risks associated with alcohol use. Alcohol ad restrictions reduce the exposure of children and adolescents to alcohol ads promoting unrealistic messages about alcohol use.
- Parents and other concerned adults cannot control young people's exposure to alcohol messages if advertising is unrestricted in public places. With alcohol ad restrictions, communities have some control over the amount of alcohol advertising that young people are exposed to.
- Public alcohol advertising often targets young people. At the very least, communities should place restrictions on the presence of advertisements such as alcohol billboards which are located near schools, churches, and residential areas. In addition, communities can place restrictions on the number of alcohol billboards in low-income neighborhoods, where the presence of such billboards is often disproportionately high.
- Communities which allow alcohol advertisers to target youth send a message to young people that underage alcohol use is tolerated by the community. Restricting alcohol advertising in public places may help change community norms regarding alcohol use and send a message to youth that underage drinking is not acceptable.

Considerations for passing this ordinance in your community:

Issue: The alcohol industry may bring lawsuits in response to ad bans or restrictions, arguing that the restrictions violate the First Amendment right to free speech.

Response: To overcome this constitutional barrier, communities must show that the potential harm to the public's health or welfare from alcohol is real enough to justify the content regulation of speech. This can be a heavy burden, but courts have recognized that alcohol, although legal, is a legitimate subject of this type of speech regulation.

Note: Community members are urged to consult with a local attorney to take into account state law requirements before attempting to pass a local ordinance.

> *"With alcohol ad restrictions, communities have some control over the amount of alcohol advertising that young people are exposed to."*

Alcohol ad restrictions and the larger context:

Passing ordinances which ban or restrict alcohol advertising in public places may help initiate community discussion around other policies which can be implemented to reduce young people's exposure to alcohol promotions, such as restrictions on alcohol sponsorships. However, policies which target alcohol promotions are not enough to reduce a community's underage drinking problem. Alcohol control policies which aim to reduce underage access through restrictions on merchant, individual, and community practices are also needed. Several such policies include:

- Compliance checks of alcohol establishments which help ensure that employees are complying with age of sale laws and to encourage outlets to monitor their employees.
- Keg registration policies which identify and penalize adults and youth who purchase kegs for parties and allow underage youth to consume the alcohol.
- Alcohol restrictions in public places which control the availability and use of alcohol in parks, beaches, and other unsupervised places where alcohol consumption by teens may be especially likely to lead to problems.

Alcohol Advertising Does Not Cause Teens to Drink

by Morris E. Chafetz

About the author: *Morris E. Chafetz is former director of the National Institute on Alcohol Abuse and Alcoholism and the author of* The Tyranny of Experts: Blowing the Whistle on the Cult of Expertise.

As a psychiatrist, scientist and former architect of the national effort to prevent alcohol problems, it was my job to seek out the best science, both biomedical and behavioral.

Today, a heated debate swirls around the issue of restricting alcohol advertising on TV. Assorted opponents who argue that advertising contributes to alcohol-related problems—especially among young people—are way off base.

When I consider the pros and cons of alcohol advertising and its alleged effect on problem drinking, I find myself asking the crucial question: Where in the name of science is there proof that alcohol advertising is bad for society?

[In 1996], I was asked to write a review for the *New England Journal of Medicine* on how advertising affects alcohol use. I did not find any studies that credibly connect advertising to increases in alcohol use (or abuse) or to young persons taking up drinking.

Distorting the Evidence

The prevalence of reckless misinterpretation and misapplication of science allows advocacy groups and the media to stretch research findings to suit their preconceived positions.

For example, one study showed that adolescents who drank alcohol could remember alcohol ads better than adolescents who did not drink. But what does that prove? If researchers found that green-colored automobiles had more accidents than cars of other colors, would that prove the color green causes accidents?

Another study, supported by the Center on Alcohol Advertising, reportedly showed that people who knew about the federal guidelines on moderate drinking drank less than people who didn't know.

Poppycock! The many variables that affect behavior and define moderate drinking are scientifically uncontrollable. Anyone with any scientific knowledge knows the study is nonsense.

But the issue of whether alcohol advertising should be restricted goes beyond what I have noted.

During our adolescent years we tested the world by taking risks, and we made it. So will the present generation of teenagers. But there endures a sturdy, albeit insecure, band of believers dedicated to the idyllic dream of the innocent, sheltered child.

The results of a national survey of high school students belie this perfect child fantasy. In the study, researchers with the Addiction Research Foundation in Ontario, Canada, found that 76 percent of 12th-graders and 69 percent of 10th-graders in the United States drank alcohol in 1996.

State surveys have shown even higher rates of consumption by young people: An analysis of four large surveys of 11th-graders in Ohio showed that 87 percent of the boys and 82 percent of the girls drank alcohol.

Teenage Drinking Is Normal

A book from England, "The Normal and the Abnormal in Adolescent Drinking," provides a realistic picture of alcohol and adolescence.

The authors contend that adolescent drinking is a normal part of the socialization process, wherein teenagers experiment with and acquire adult behavior. The high incidence of adolescent drinking buttresses this argument. But the authors further contend that adolescent abstinence is as deviant as excessive drinking. I agree with their position.

Abstinence and excessive drinking are unhealthy extremes. Neither behavior should be encouraged, for in the real world, drinking alcohol in moderation is socially acceptable.

The idea of considering teenage abstinence abnormal will shock most Americans. But evidence that most 10th-, 11th- and 12th-graders in the United States drank some alcohol last year suggests that abstinence is indeed abnormal in this age group. Thus, the goal of abstinence for adolescents is unrealistic.

Advocacy groups claim, without evidence, that alcohol advertising encourages young people to drink. With such an easy target as alcoholic beverages, evidence seems unnecessary. And the lust to blame something or someone for youthful waywardness is so intense that parents can be held legally responsible for their children's wanton acts.

Trying to lend young people a helping hand is exemplary. But in their zeal, child-protection advocates may be contributing to the problems they work so hard to prevent. The cult of expertise has made parents feel incapable of raising their children. But as a parent and psychiatrist, I trust the instincts of parents more than I do the hubris of child-protection experts.

Alcohol Advertising Does Not Affect Alcohol Consumption

by the Advertising Association

About the author: *The Advertising Association is a trade organization in the United Kingdom that represents advertising agencies and related media services.*

In spite of the proven success of advertising regulation and the responsible attitude of the advertising industry, there is criticism about alcohol advertising, especially in relation to its presumed impact on consumption and abusive consumption. Such criticism is, more often than not, based on a lack of understanding about the role of advertising and confusion between "brand advertising" and "generic advertising".

In general, companies advertise their own brands in order to increase the overall market share of their brands alone and to protect that market share against brand switching by consumers. Brand advertising, of the type seen in the alcoholic drinks market sector, is a tool of competition between brands, not a means to ensure overall increases in total consumption of a product type.

Advertising and Consumption: The Research Findings

Moreover, there is no relationship between responsible brand advertising in the alcoholic drinks sector and the misuse of the product itself. The causal factors related to alcohol abuse are many. They include social, economic, demographic and perhaps genetic influences upon which brand advertising has little or no impact. Restrictions on advertising will not reduce or eliminate misuse as the experience of countries in which bans have been imposed shows. According to a paper entitled "The Drinking Revolution: Building a Campaign for Safer Drinking", published by Alcohol Concern in 1987: "There is little or no evidence that advertising increases total consumption of alcohol as against increasing a particular product's share of the market."

Reprinted, with permission, from "Alcohol Advertising," an executive brief published by the Advertising Association, December 19, 2000, at www.adassoc.org.uk/briefs/alc.htm.

Per capita consumption of alcohol is lower today in Europe than it has been for most of the past three centuries. In addition, the UK actually has lower rates of "officially recorded" consumption than almost any other country in Western Europe, other than the Scandinavian countries and Iceland, where high taxes and national alcohol policies have led to very high levels of unrecorded consumption. France, where an ad ban has been in place since 1991, continues to have a very high level of alcohol consumption and is in second place in the Western Europe per capita alcohol consumption league.

The US Federal Trade Commission's (FTC) Bureaux of Consumer Protection & Economics undertook a review of the available literature on alcohol advertising and consumption in 1985. This extensive government survey of the literature concerning the general effects of advertising reached conclusions that were further confirmed by similar FTC appraisals directed specifically at the alcoholic drinks sector. The review of evidence concluded that: "The large majority of such studies found little or no effect of advertising on total industry demand."

A study by Chiplin, Sturgess and Dunning in 1981 also concluded that: "It remains unproven that advertising has led to any marked increase in aggregate demand in general, or in the demand for . . . alcohol. . . . It must be recognised that advertising could well be the wrong target in seeking to curtail consumption of products such as . . . alcohol. . . . It does appear that so far there is little convincing support for the argument that changes in total consumption of these products are caused by advertising."

A more recent independent review of the available literature carried out by Calfee and Scheraga in 1989 concluded that: "Econometric and laboratory research in the US, Canada and the UK have not revealed advertising to have a significant effect on alcohol consumption. The same is true of survey research which confirms the powerful role of social factors such as the attitudes and behaviour of parents and peers."

The authors go on to say that: "The data shows that social forces other than prices and income were bringing about a strong reduction in demand for alcoholic beverages and that advertising did nothing to ward off this trend."

One study, published in 1981, has been quoted by many observers as demonstrating a link between advertising and consumption. This study was Atkin & Block: "Content and Effects of Alcohol Advertising", National Technical Information Service (USA) 1981. However, in April 1992, Dr

> *"Restrictions on advertising will not reduce or eliminate [alcohol] misuse."*

Block submitted evidence to a US Senate Subcommittee which included the following reference to his 1981 study: "This study does not demonstrate that exposure to alcohol advertising causes consumption of alcohol that would not otherwise occur. . . . Most importantly, from my review of the scientific literature, I can find no persuasive evidence that advertising causes non-drinkers to start drinking or that advertising causes drinkers to become abusers . . . if anything the advertisements we studied would reinforce only moderate consumption. . . ."

Although these remarks referred to the findings of Dr Block from US sources, many of the ads described were produced by advertisers and agencies who market and advertise the same or similar brands in Europe and follow similar self-regulatory codes.

France's Alcohol Advertising Restrictions

Many organizations calling for tighter restrictions on alcoholic drinks advertising cite the example of France as providing substantiation for their arguments.

Per capita alcohol consumption in France had peaked during the mid 1950s. The decline that followed was halted briefly in the early 1970s only to resume even more strongly in the latter part of that decade. It should be noted that in spite of this decline, France continues to have one of the highest rates of alcohol consumption in Europe. At first these reductions in French consumption were driven by the increased availability of clean drinking water. Then changing lifestyles took over. Adults began to drop the habit of drinking liqueurs after dinner. Younger consumers gradually abandoned the traditional French preference for wine with every meal and adopted the more international preference for beer, soft drinks and "lighter products" generally.

In 1991 the French Government implemented the Loi Evin [Evin Law] with the explicit purpose of reducing the health costs of alcohol abuse. The law severely restricts alcoholic drinks advertising.

The downward slide in consumption continued through 1994 virtually as it had in the fifteen years before the Loi Evin was enacted, despite the fact that advertising declined precipitously after the law was passed.

> *"At most, advertising has a statistically insignificant effect on [alcohol] consumption."*

In 1997, John E Calfee (Resident Scholar at the American Enterprise Institute for Public Policy Research, Washington DC) revisited the issue of advertising and consumption in his book entitled "Fear of Persuasion: A New Perspective on Advertising and Regulation". Calfee examined the situation within France and concluded that: "Statistical analysis confirmed that advertising has had no discernible effect in increasing French total alcohol consumption above what it would otherwise have been. Of course market shares have shifted (wine's share has fallen dramatically for example) and advertising is presumably a factor in those shifts. But advertising has had no detectable effect in the deeper issue of how much drinking occurs overall."

More recently, a new survey of alcohol consumption in France by the French Health Education Authority has found that French teenagers are actually smoking and drinking more per year since 1991, the year in which the ban on alcohol and tobacco advertising was introduced. Furthermore, since the imposition of the Loi Evin, a competitive new market for low priced high strength own label beer has emerged. This category (now sold in supermarkets and apparently drunk by those "seeking inebriation") increased by no less than 33% between 1991 and 1996. Over the same period, alcohol consumption by teenagers has actually increased—the opposite of what was intended.

No Evidence to Support Advertising Restrictions

Independent, academic research based on statistical evidence and taking into account prices, incomes, sales and ad-spend illustrates that, at most, advertising has a statistically insignificant effect on consumption. There is little or no overall impact on total category consumption as a result of brand advertising. This would reinforce the argument put forward by the advertising industry that in a mature market such as alcoholic drinks, advertising is targeted to reinforce brand identity, offset brand-switching and maintain market share rather than encourage greater levels of overall consumption across the category.

> *"Responsible advertising is the norm in the alcoholic drinks sector."*

Evidence from countries in which advertising bans have been imposed show that, contrary to the arguments put forward by some lobbying organizations, these bans have little or no effect on reducing consumption, particularly among target groups such as young people.

The current regulatory structures in the UK are working well and are regularly reviewed to take into account perceived problems and changes in public opinion. Responsible advertising is the norm in the alcoholic drinks sector and compliance with existing regulations is high.

Those organizations that continue to portray restrictions on advertising as a panacea for the problems associated with alcohol misuse, whilst undoubtedly well-intentioned, are mistaken in their belief that restricting legitimate freedom of speech is a credible addition or alternative to a logical anti-misuse strategy.

The Alcohol Industry Has the Right to Advertise Its Products

by Doug Bandow

About the author: *Doug Bandow is a senior fellow at the Cato Institute, a conservative think tank in Washington, D.C., that promotes individual liberty and limited government.*

Puritans have long been viewed as people who couldn't stand the thought of anyone anywhere having a good time. The original Puritans really weren't that way, but, today, the world seems full of such killjoys.

For instance, in Dallas, the local Starplex amphitheater has sold naming rights to United Distillers & Vintners (UDV), a unit of Britain's Diageo PLC that controls one-fifth of the U.S. distilled spirits market. Local activists are in an uproar.

A multitude of stadiums and other entertainment facilities have sold their identities. As did the 20,000-seat music complex, Dallas' largest, which for 10 years was known as Coca-Cola Starplex. But Coke ended its sponsorship in 1998, so the House of Blues and SFX Entertainment Inc. recently inked an eight-year deal with UDV to call the Starplex the Smirnoff Music Centre.

From the subsequent popular reaction, one would think that a bunch of Colombian druglords had taken over the city. Dallas City Councilman Leo Chaney told the *Dallas Morning News*: "My first reaction is to organize the community and picket and protest in front of the Starplex."

A Legal Product

Exactly why is hard to fathom. Chaney complained that the name countered the attempt "to deal with the perception that the South Dallas/Fair Park area is overrun by liquor establishments."

Yet, the area where the Starplex is located either is or isn't so overrun. The Centre's name is irrelevant.

Reprinted from "Alcohol Supersensitivity," by Doug Bandow, *Cato Today's Commentary*, July 18, 2000. Reprinted by permission of the Cato Institute.

A number of other people complained about the "message." One parent said simply: "I don't think they ought to name a facility with something that everybody associates with alcohol."

But alcohol is legal to sell. It is legal to advertise. It is legal to drink. What, then, is wrong with putting the name of Smirnoff, an alcoholic beverage, on a building?

Adults have a right to learn about the availability of a legal product. There's no difference in principle among advertising in a magazine, on television, through a billboard or with a building's name.

Moreover, there's no reason to believe that any of these is likely to create a surge in drinking. Most people don't have to be lobbied to enjoy alcohol. They do have to be prodded to choose a particular maker's brand. Thus, the Smirnoff Music Centre is more likely to affect brand preferences than consumption levels.

Interestingly, in the Centre Smirnoff liquor will be available only to members of two private clubs. The public concessionaires just sell beer and wine.

"Protecting Children"

The last refuge of the Texas Puritans is that some children will see the name. By that logic nothing unavailable to children smoking cigarettes, making contracts, driving autos, getting tattoos, going bungee jumping should be advertised anywhere, anytime. If even one child is present, everyone should be treated as a child.

That, of course, would eliminate the illusion that we live in a free society. The goal should not be to hide from minors images of the rights of adulthood, but to prepare children to exercise those rights intelligently when they become adults.

Indeed, UDV does not advertise to audiences with less than 70 percent adults. Fewer than one-in-10 Starplex attendees are under 21. Moreover, UDV doesn't plan on including images of Smirnoff bottles at the Centre.

Given the controversy, one might think that Smirnoff was the first entertainment facility to be named after an alcohol producer. However, the names Bud Light, Busch, Coors, and Molson adorn amphitheaters and stadiums in several cities.

A similar controversy erupted several years ago when Seagram's announced that it planned on advertising whiskey on television. Critics streamed forth while ignoring the beer advertising that pervades TV.

Yet alcohol is alcohol: all standard drinks include roughly the same amount of alcohol, 14.5 grams. The 12-ounce bottle of Smirnoff Ice is 5 percent alcohol by volume, the same as a 12-ounce bottle of beer.

"The goal should not be to hide from minors images of the rights of adulthood, but to prepare children to exercise those rights intelligently when they become adults."

If the Dallas protesters were really serious, they should attack other Starplex sponsors. There is, after all, Coors Brewing Co., which sells, yes, alcohol. Ben & Jerry's, which foists cholesterol-rich ice cream on America's overweight population. And the Texas Lottery, which inveigles poor people to waste their money on the ripoff that masquerades as state-sponsored gambling.

Almost any good thing in life can be abused. So it is with alcohol.

A Responsible Company

But UDV has attempted to minimize such problems, participating in a number of industry and community initiatives that address drunken and underage driving. There is nothing to suggest that UDV is anything other than a responsible provider of a perfectly moral and legal product.

It's hard to know whether the Smirnoff Music Centre is worth the $6 million spent by UDV. But that is the company's problem. UDV has a right to buy the naming rights to the amphitheater.

Freedom is precious. Among its greatest enemies are well-intended busybodies who desire to treat the rest of us like children. If they succeed, we will all lose.

The Alcohol Industry Works to Discourage Underage Drinking

by Cheryl Ursin

About the author: *Cheryl Ursin is a contributing editor to* Beverage Dynamics, *a prominent beverage industry trade magazine.*

"Working together, we've made enormous progress in reducing drunk driving in America," said President Clinton in a [fall 1999] radio address. "Last year, the number of people killed in alcohol-related crashes hit a record low; and young people killed in alcohol-related crashes fell to the lowest rate ever recorded."

The latest data available from the National Highway Traffic Safety Administration (NHTSA) shows that alcohol-related fatalities in car crashes declined by 33% in the 10-year period between 1988 and 1998.

Meanwhile, according to a 1999 survey by the Department of Health & Human Services, the percentage of teenagers, ages 12 to 17, who reported having had a drink in the previous month was 45% lower in 1998 than it was in 1982.

Things Are Getting Better

But, strangely, not everyone seems to have heard this news. A recent survey by the National Beer Wholesalers Association showed that the majority of respondents thought there were more drunk drivers on the road and more underage drinking going on than ever before.

"One of the things we have to focus on is getting the message out that things are getting better," said Jeff Becker, president of the Beer Institute, a trade association for the American brewing industry. "This has been a tremendous public-health success."

Still, in a speech to the National Licensed Beverage Association in January [2000], Peter Coors, president and CEO of Coors, said, "We're far from out of the woods, and I would argue that there may never be an end to this fight—that constant vigilance and action to discourage irresponsible consumption of beer, wine and spirits are an integral part of the business."

Beverage alcohol suppliers and their trade associations have taken responsible consumption education, research and legislation very seriously—and have done so for many years. For example, the Century Council, a national, not-for-profit organization funded by America's leading distillers, has spent over $100 million to combat alcohol abuse in the eight years of its existence. Individually, suppliers have also traditionally educated their consumers about responsible consumption. As early as 1937, for example, Seagram ran an ad that proclaimed, "Drinking and driving do not mix." And last September [1999], Anheuser-Busch announced that it was nearly tripling its investment in efforts to combat alcohol abuse. Its new advertising campaign will have a $40 million media budget. "Rather than declare victory and stop," said Francine Katz, vice president of consumer affairs at the brewing company, "it's time to recognize what works and do more."

So, what does work?

When it comes to underage drinking, on the one hand, the situation is improving. According to the NHTSA, fatalities in crashes involving drunk teenagers declined by 65% from 1982 to 1998. But, on the other hand, combating underage drinking is a constantly evolving challenge. With each new generation of children, the process has to start all over again.

Educating Children and Parents

And as anyone who has ever shopped with a teenager knows, teenage culture changes rapidly. "Drinking has always been a part of the social scene on college campuses," said John Lawn, chairman and CEO of the Century Council, who has over 20 years of experience in law enforcement, including a five-year stint as the head of the Drug Enforcement Administration (DEA). "In 1800, Harvard celebrated George Washington's birthday with alcohol on campus. But now, it's different even from how it was when I was in college." He pointed out that it is different for younger children as well. "When I was a kid, my friends and I might get hold of some cans of beer at 16," he said. "Now, kids begin experimenting at a much younger age, at 10."

The changes in childhood and teenage culture mean changes in the methods used to teach about alcohol. For children ages 10 to 14, the Century Council has partnered with the Boys & Girls Clubs of America to administer a program called "Ready or Not: Talking to Kids About Alcohol." The program, which includes a video available as a "free rental" from Blockbuster video stores, encourages adults to discuss alcohol with children at an age when

> *"Constant vigilance and action to discourage irresponsible consumption of beer, wine and spirits are an integral part of the business."*

many will be confronted with their first decisions about drinking.

Companies and organizations offer a wide range of programs designed to educate children and their parents, from Beginning Alcohol and Addictions Basic Education Studies (BAABES)—a program targeted at kids ages 3 to 12, funded in part by the Beer Institute and now operating in 45 states—to Alcohol 101, an interactive CD-ROM developed for use with college students by the University of Illinois in collaboration with the Century Council and now in use at more than 1,600 colleges and universities nationwide.

Targeting Binge Drinking

Within the realm of underage drinking, drinking on college campuses, especially binge drinking, has been of special concern. A study done by the Harvard School of Public Health in 1997 found that 43% of college students were binge drinkers, a binge being defined as having five or more drinks, if male, or four or more drinks, if female, in one sitting.

In addition to Alcohol 101, the Century Council created a book, called *Promising Practices: Campus Alcohol Strategies*, by contacting every one of the approximately 3,800 colleges and universities in the U.S., having a board of educators review each one's alcohol-abuse prevention strategies and then profiling over 200 of the most effective.

> *"When it comes to underage drinking . . . the situation is improving."*

Brewers have also targeted college students. Anheuser-Busch, Coors and Miller, for example, are among the sponsors of the National Collegiate Alcohol Awareness Week every year in October.

And of course, suppliers of all types work with retailers to help prevent sales to underage consumers. The Century Council, for example, still runs its very successful Cops in Shops program, in which local police officers pose as clerks in liquor stores, in 44 states. According to a recent survey by the National Association of Governors' Highway Safety Representatives, alcoholic beverage control agents in states where the program was in use rated its effectiveness as a 10 out of 10. Meanwhile, brewers, the Beer Institute and the National Beer Wholesalers Association provide a variety of booklets and laminated cards, some available in several languages, designed to assist retailers in spotting fake IDs.

Industry Support for Drunk Driving Legislation

While the number of drunk-driving incidents in general has been declining for several years, suppliers and others who try to prevent drunk driving still face their toughest challenge. Basically, while social drinkers have heeded the responsibility messages they see, the worst kind of drunk driver, often referred to as the "hard-core drunk driver," has yet to be reached. And currently, it is these drivers—who repeatedly drive with blood alcohol content (BAC) levels far above the legal limit—who cause half of all alcohol-related car accidents. Some experts say that not only are a third of those who are arrested for drunk driving repeat offenders but that most of them have driven drunk thousands of times in their lifetimes.

"We have reached the point where to make the next substantial impact, we must deal with the hard-core drunk driver," said Lawn of the Century Council. Advertisements and educational campaigns do not work with these problem drinkers. Often, in fact, laws don't either. "If they're stopped and given a citation, or even if their licenses are removed, they will continue to drive," said Lawn.

Many suppliers back legislation designed to deal with these hard-core drunk drivers. In February [2000], for example, John Bowlin, president and chief executive officer of Miller Brewing Company, testified in support of a bill in Wisconsin which proposed stiffer penalties and improved treatment programs for repeat offenders. The bill has since been passed. Meanwhile, Coors has supported legislation targeted at hard-core drunk drivers in nearly 30 states in 1999.

When President Clinton gave his radio address, he was doing so to announce that the Departments of Transportation and Justice had just released over $47 million in grants to combat the problems of drunk driving and underage drinking.

Anheuser-Busch's new advertising campaign sums it up the best, perhaps. It's entitled, "We All Make A Difference." And the beverage alcohol industry continues to do its part—supporting legislation, funding research and taking its messages of responsible consumption to the public.

Chapter 4

Are Age-21 Laws Effective in Reducing Teen Alcohol Abuse?

The Drinking Age Debate: An Overview

by Deborah Straszheim

About the author: *Deborah Straszheim is a reporter for the* Newport News *(Virginia)* Daily Press.

It used to be no big deal. Associate Professor Donald Baxter would invite students to his house to talk politics and have cokes, soda, or beer.

That was before the drinking age was 21. He knows that back then, bad things sometimes happened on college campuses, just like they do today. But it's hard to remember much bad at the College of William and Mary. "It almost seemed a healthier situation," said Baxter.

[In 1998] he went to a campus social event that had separate areas for the 21 and under 21 crowd. It was, Baxter says, strange.

"The adults could go in this room, and the children, the students, could go in this other room. It was kind of artificial," he said.

Faculty and administrators, not just at William and Mary but in colleges elsewhere in Virginia, have mixed feelings about the rules and the age limit they're working with. It's not that they think it's OK for students to get drunk or that they won't back their universities. They simply have different ideas about how to best encourage responsible behavior.

Lower the Drinking Age?

Some believe students were better off when the drinking age was 18.

"Then you could talk about it. You could actually do something about changing drinking behavior when it was legal," said Thomas Goodale, a nationally recognized expert on college alcohol use and the author of books on the subject.

[In November 1998] a disagreement over how to deal with college student parties became apparent during a meeting of William and Mary's board of visitors.

Three board members, including William Barr, a former U.S. Attorney General known for his tough stance on crime, criticized a rule that requires students to be on a guest list before they may attend any event where alcohol is served.

Barr called the rule idiotic because he said it wrecked spontaneity but didn't stop underage drinking. He wasn't addressing the drinking age, but his comments served to highlight the difficulties colleges face in dealing with alcohol use.

Clay Clemens, associate professor of government at W&M, said the problem with alcohol seems about the same as it was when the drinking age was 18.

But today, he said, colleges are in an awkward position in the war on alcohol abuse. They must uphold the law without exception due to the explosive climate, but also be reasonable.

"The law is 25 miles per hour on roads. Do we slap a fine on everyone who goes 26?" he said.

Sam Sadler, vice president for student affairs at W&M, said the balance is difficult. But the college will keep at it.

"Students will say, quite often, that the culture sends them mixed messages," Sadler said. "They'll say, 'I'm old enough to be drafted, to vote for the president of the United States, to incur financial debt. And you're telling me I can't have a beer? And on top of that, if I do, now you're going to call my parents?'"

"What I hear coming out of colleges is the solution is going to be lowering the drinking age," said Terrance Schiavone, president of the National Commission Against Drunk Driving. "Then there will be less control, and more drinking going on. All they're going to have are more problems."

A Decrease in Drunk Driving

The drinking age changed from 18 to 21 in many states under President Reagan in the mid-1980s. When Reagan signed the National Minimum Drinking Age Act of 1984, any state that failed to pass an age-21 law within two years risked losing its federal highway money. All 50 states complied.

The result, according to supporters of the law, was a reduction in alcohol-related traffic deaths.

"What's really changed is that we finally have awakened to the seriousness of it," said William DeJong, director of U.S. Department of Education's Higher Education Center for Alcohol and Other Drug Prevention, a national organization that advises colleges on drug and alcohol policies.

If some folks think students should be allowed to drink at 18, they're "dead wrong," he said.

The National Highway Traffic Safety Administration has estimated 16,000 lives have been saved as a result of states that adopted a 21 age before or after the national law, he said.

> *"Colleges are in an awkward position in the war on alcohol abuse."*

DeJong also cited a study by a University of Minnesota researcher that found that young people living in states with a 21 age limit started drinking later and drank more moderately than those in states with a younger age.

He said colleges may find it difficult to have students on both sides of the drinking age; but it's better than the alternative.

"I would much rather have people in college deal with that problem than people in high school," DeJong said. "Right now, you have a senior in college buying alcohol for his friends who are sophomores. That's much better than having a senior in high school buying alcohol for his friends."

Schiavone, who once worked as a police officer in Massachusetts, agreed.

"I'm of the mind that 21, though maybe not perfect age, is an age that this country basically has gotten used to. If we enforced it better, we would probably even save more lives," he said. DeJong co-wrote a study published earlier this year on alcohol-related traffic deaths since 1988.

Many Teens Ignore the Age Limit

Goodale said he doesn't believe in the statistics supporting a 21 age. There may be other reasons for the reductions in traffic fatalities, such as safer roads, he said. He said students start drinking long before 21 even with the age limit.

The number of students cited for alcohol infractions peaks at ninth grade in Virginia, when students are typically 15 or 16, he noted.

A [1998] Harvard School of Public Health College Alcohol Study . . . showed binge drinking has continued unabated for the past four years. The study was based on the responses of 14,500 students from 116 colleges nationwide, and reported a small drop in binge drinking (defined as five or more drinks in one sitting) because more students do not drink at all.

"There are no national statistics available on how many college students die from alcohol-related causes today compared to when the drinking age was 18."

This was offset by more intense drinking among students who did drink—more drinking to get drunk, the study said.

Baxter, of William and Mary, said life has become much more complicated than it was in the days when students could legally drink and mingle with faculty.

It may not have been perfect, but it seemed more normal, he said.

"Kids are going to drink something one way or another. When you make a law of 21, then you sort of criminalize what is, for this age group, normal behavior," he said.

"It means that the whole drinking scene has to go underground."

When students hide their drinking there is no one to advise, oversee, or say it's time to stop, college officials said.

Reducing Alcohol Abuse Is the Goal

There are no national statistics available on how many college students die from alcohol-related causes today compared to when the drinking age was 18,

"Students go through this, but the fact is, it doesn't have to be this way at all," DeJong said. "There is nothing about adolescence that requires people to drink to the extremes that we are seeing."

Others said that may be true, but today's focus doesn't seem right either.

"To me it seems that the focus is all on the wrong thing," said Clemens. "It should be on keeping people out of cars, instead of keeping a 19-year-old from having a Budweiser."

Raising the Drinking Age to 21 Has Reduced Alcohol-Related Injuries and Death Among Youth

by Traci L. Toomey, Carolyn Rosenfeld, and Alexander C. Wagenaar

About the authors: *At the time this article was written, Traci L. Toomey was a research associate with, Carolyn Rosenfeld was a recent graduate of, and Alexander C. Wagenaar was a professor at the University of Minnesota, Division of Epidemiology.*

Science can play a critical role in developing effective policies to address health issues, including those focused on alcohol-related problems. In an ideal world, public policy development would be based on the identification of a problem and the scientific evidence of the factors that are most effective in reducing that problem. In the real world, however, public policy results from economic and political forces, which occasionally combine with good science. Minimum legal drinking age (MLDA) laws provide an example of how scientific research can support effective public policies. This article shows how science has influenced MLDA policies in the past and summarizes research contributing to the ongoing debate on the MLDA.

History of the MLDA

Following the repeal of Prohibition, nearly all State laws restricting youth access to alcohol designated 21 as the minimum age for purchasing and consuming alcohol. Between 1970 and 1975, however, 29 States lowered the MLDA to age 18, 19, or 20. These changes occurred at the same time that minimum-age limits for other activities, such as voting, also were being lowered. Scientists began studying the effects of the lowered MLDA, particularly focusing on traf-

Excerpted from "The Minimum Legal Drinking Age: History, Effectiveness, and Ongoing Debate," by Traci L. Toomey, Carolyn Rosenfeld, and Alexander C. Wagenaar, in *Alcohol Health and Research World*, vol. 20, no. 4, 1996. Reprinted with permission.

fic crashes, the leading cause of death among teenagers. Several studies in the 1970's showed that traffic crashes increased significantly among teenagers after the MLDA was lowered.

With evidence that lower legal drinking ages were associated with more traffic crashes among youth, citizen advocacy groups led a movement to restore the MLDA to 21 in all States. In response, 16 States increased their MLDA's between September 1976 and January 1983. Many States, however, resisted pressure from these groups and ignored Government incentives to raise their MLDA's. The Federal Government became concerned about the safety both of youth in States that had lower MLDA's and of youth who lived in neighboring States. Persons who were below the MLDA in their own State could drive across State borders to purchase alcohol in a State with a lower MLDA and then return home, increasing the likelihood of being involved in traffic crashes.

Because the 21st amendment to the U.S. Constitution guaranteed States' rights to regulate alcohol, the Federal Government could not mandate a uniform MLDA of 21. Instead, in 1984 the Federal Government passed the Uniform Drinking Age Act, which provided for a decrease in Federal highway funding to States that did not establish an MLDA of 21 by 1987. Faced with a loss of funding, the remaining States returned their MLDA's to age 21 by 1988.

Reductions in Drinking

Following the end of Prohibition, each State developed its own set of policies to regulate the distribution, sale, and consumption of alcohol. In addition to the MLDA, examples of other alcohol control policies include excise taxes, restrictions on hours and days of sales, and server training. Many of these other alcohol policies have only recently been evaluated. Of all the alcohol control policies, MLDA policy has been the most studied. Since the 1970's, at least 70 studies have explicitly examined the effects of either increases or decreases in the MLDA, with some studies using more robust research designs than others. MLDA policies may have been evaluated sooner and more often for a variety of reasons, including: (1) a growing concern about youth drinking and driving; (2) availability of archived, time-series data on traffic crashes; (3) the fact that many States first lowered, then raised, their MLDA's; and (4) preliminary research showing the large effects of changes in MLDA's. . . . MLDA laws have been evaluated mostly in terms of how changing the MLDA affects rates of alcohol use and traffic crashes among youth.

"Reduced rates of alcohol use among youth after the MLDA was increased were primarily evident in decreased rates of beer consumption."

Methods used to study the effect of the MLDA on alcohol use have varied widely, contributing to differences in conclusions among studies. For example, some studies used convenience samples, such as students in introductory psychology classes, whereas other studies used sophisticated, random sampling designs to obtain nationally representative samples. [Researcher A.C.] Wagenaar concluded that studies employing strong research and analytical designs typically observed increases in alcohol use among youth following a lowering of the MLDA. In contrast, when many States raised the MLDA, alcohol use among youth decreased.

Beer is the alcoholic beverage of choice for most youth. As a result, reduced rates of alcohol use among youth after the MLDA was increased were primarily evident in decreased rates of beer consumption. Rates of wine and distilled spirits use among youth did not change dramatically following the rise in the MLDA.

Opponents of the age-21 MLDA theorized that even if a higher MLDA reduced alcohol use among minors, drinking rates and alcohol-related problems would surge among those age 21 and older. In other words, opponents believed that a "rubber band" effect would occur: When youth turned 21, they would drink to "make up for lost time" and thus drink at higher rates than they would had they been allowed to drink alcohol at an earlier age. A study by P.M. O'Malley and A.C. Wagenaar, however, refutes this theory. Using a national probability sample, O'Malley and Wagenaar found that the lower rates of alcohol use due to a high legal drinking age continued even after youth turned 21.

Although the MLDA's effect on youth alcohol consumption is important, a key consideration is whether the MLDA ultimately affects the rates of alcohol-related problems. Alcohol use among youth is related to

> *"In 1987 alone, 1,071 traffic crash fatalities were prevented because of the MLDA of 21."*

numerous problems, including traffic crashes, drownings, vandalism, assaults, homicides, suicides, teenage pregnancies, and sexually transmitted diseases. Alcohol use is reported in one-fifth to two-thirds of many of these problems. As drinking rates increase or decrease, rates of alcohol-related problems may change in response.

Decreases in Traffic Crashes

Using various research methods, at least 50 studies have evaluated the effect of changes in the MLDA on traffic crashes. Some studies assessed policy changes in only one State, whereas others analyzed the MLDA's effect across multiple States. These studies evaluated the effect of MLDA changes on a variety of outcomes, including total traffic crash fatalities for youth; drinking-driving convictions; crashes resulting in injuries; and single-vehicle nighttime crash fatalities (the crashes most likely to involve alcohol).

Most studies on the effect of lowering the MLDA found an increase in traffic crashes and traffic deaths among youth. Of the 29 studies completed since the early 1980's that evaluated increases in the MLDA, 20 showed significant decreases in traffic crashes and crash fatalities. Only three clearly found no change in traffic crashes involving youth. The remaining six studies had equivocal results. Based on results from research studies such as these, the National Highway Traffic Safety Administration (NHTSA) estimated that in 1987 alone, 1,071 traffic crash fatalities were prevented because of the MLDA of 21.

Since 1984 researchers have been investigating whether changes in the MLDA also affect other alcohol-related problems. Of the four studies conducted to date that focused on other social and health consequences of alcohol use, three found an inverse relationship between the MLDA and alcohol-related problems: A higher legal drinking age was correlated

> *"The MLDA of 21 saves the lives of well over 1,000 youth each year."*

with a lower number of alcohol problems among youth. The New York State Division of Alcoholism and Alcohol Abuse found a 16-percent decrease in rates of vandalism in four States that raised the MLDA. In a study of an increase of the MLDA in Massachusetts, R. Hingson and colleagues did not find significant changes in the rates of nonmotor-vehicle trauma, suicide, or homicide. D.I. Smith, however, found an increase in non-traffic-related hospital admissions following decreases in the MLDA in two Australian states. N.E. Jones and colleagues found lower rates of death caused by suicides, motor vehicle crashes, pedestrian accidents, and other injuries in States with higher MLDA's. More research is needed to characterize the full effect of the MLDA on rates of alcohol-related injuries and on problems other than motor vehicle crashes.

Making the MLDA Even More Effective

Research indicates that a higher MLDA results in fewer alcohol-related problems among youth and that the MLDA of 21 saves the lives of well over 1,000 youth each year. What is compelling is that the effect of the higher MLDA is occurring with little or no enforcement. A common argument among opponents of a higher MLDA is that because many minors still drink and purchase alcohol, an MLDA of 21 does not work. The evidence shows, however, that although many youth still consume alcohol, they drink less and experience fewer alcohol-related injuries and deaths than they did under lower MLDA's. A more appropriate discussion, therefore, is not whether the MLDA should again be lowered but whether the current MLDA can be made even more effective.

Despite laws prohibiting the sale or provision of alcohol to people under age 21, minors throughout the United States can easily obtain alcohol from many sources. Buyers who appear to be younger than 21 can successfully purchase alcohol from licensed establishments without showing age identification in 50 percent or more of their attempts. In addition, although many youth purchase alcohol themselves, most youth indicate that they generally obtain alcohol through social contacts over age 21. These social contacts—who include friends, siblings, parents, coworkers, and strangers approached outside of alcohol establishments—purchase alcohol and then either provide or sell it to minors.

Better Enforcement Is Needed

Commercial establishments licensed to sell alcohol, as well as social sources, face potential criminal penalties, fines, license suspensions, and lawsuits for selling or providing alcohol to minors. So why do they still supply alcohol to youth? One reason is that policies are not actively enforced. For policies to deter specific behaviors effectively, people must believe that they have some chance of being caught and that they will face swift consequences for noncompliance. M. Wolfson and colleagues found that only 38 percent of the alcohol merchants they surveyed thought it was likely that they would be cited for selling alcohol to a minor. Further research is needed to determine whether social sources are aware of their legal liability for providing alcohol to youth and whether they perceive a high likelihood of facing penalties for doing so.

Laws prohibiting the sale and provision of alcohol to minors are not well enforced, and systems for enforcing the legislation vary by State. Typically, however, enforcement systems use both State administrative agencies, usually called State Alcohol Beverage Control (ABC) agencies, and local law enforcement agencies, such as police departments and county sheriffs. Enforcement of MLDA laws has focused primarily on penalizing underage drinkers for illegal alcohol possession or consumption, an unintended and unanticipated consequence of the MLDA. For every 1,000 minors arrested for alcohol possession, only 130 establishments that sell alcohol to them have actions taken against them, and only 88 adults who purchase alcohol for minors face criminal penalties. A.C. Wagenaar and M. Wolfson estimate that only 5 of every 100,000 incidents of minors' drinking result in a fine, license revocation, or license suspension of an alcohol establishment.

An in-depth review of enforcement actions in 295 counties in 4 States (Kentucky, Michigan, Montana, and Oregon) showed that in a 3-year period, 27 percent of the counties took no action against licensed establishments for selling alcohol to minors, and 41 percent of those counties made no arrests of adults who provided alcohol to minors. The States were selected for their diversity of alcohol-control systems and availability of data. Although the majority of counties took at least one action against alcohol establishments and adults who provided alcohol to youth, many did not take actions frequently.

> *"Laws prohibiting the sale and provision of alcohol to minors are not well enforced."*

As noted earlier, only a tiny proportion of incidents of minors' drinking results in fines or other penalties for establishments that sell alcohol. Some reasons that enforcement agencies do not cite or arrest illegal providers include (1) perceived acceptance of underage drinking by community members, (2) lack of community encouragement to increase enforcement of the MLDA, and (3) lack of resources.

Given the low level of enforcement activity, it is not surprising that many adults do not hesitate to sell or give alcohol to minors. To create a deterrent effect, we need to increase the likelihood of facing negative consequences for illegally selling or providing alcohol to youth. One approach is to encourage ABC and local law enforcement agencies to increase enforcement against illegal alcohol providers. . . .

In addition to increasing enforcement of the MLDA, other procedures and policies can be implemented to improve the effectiveness of MLDA laws. To ensure that adults do not sell or provide alcohol to minors, both public and institutional policies can

> *"As the MLDA's were lowered, rates of injuries and deaths increased; when the MLDA's were raised, injuries and deaths significantly decreased."*

be developed that complement MLDA laws. Alcohol establishments, for example, can implement several policies and practices, including (1) requiring all alcohol servers to receive responsible service training on how to check age identification and refuse sales to teenagers, (2) establishing systems to monitor servers to prevent illegal sales to youth, and (3) posting warning signs. M. Wolfson and colleagues found that establishments adhering to these policies were less likely to sell alcohol to young women who appeared to be under age 21 and who did not present age identification.

The Ongoing MLDA Debate

Despite an abundance of research demonstrating the effectiveness of the age-21 MLDA at saving lives and reducing alcohol-related problems, several States are again considering lowering their legal age limits for drinking. Louisiana's MLDA of 21 was recently challenged in court on the premise that it violates the State's constitutional law regarding age discrimination. Louisiana's State Supreme Court concluded, however, that ". . . statutes establishing the minimum drinking age at a level higher than the age of majority are not arbitrary because they substantially further the appropriate governmental purpose of improving highway safety, and thus are constitutional." In other words, because the MLDA was based on empirical evidence that such laws saved lives, the court decided that the law was not arbitrary and thus did not violate Louisiana's constitution. Despite the Louisiana decision, the MLDA of 21 also may be challenged in other States.

The same arguments used to lower the MLDA 20 years ago are being used today. Despite ongoing debates about the MLDA, research demonstrates the effectiveness of a higher MLDA in preventing alcohol-related injuries and deaths among youth. As the MLDA's were lowered, rates of injuries and deaths increased; when the MLDA's were raised, injuries and deaths significantly decreased. The benefit of using environmental (i.e., external) approaches, such as the MLDA, is further supported by the fact that drinking rates were reduced even after youth turned age 21. In contrast, individual approaches (e.g., school-based programs) have generated only short-term reductions in underage drinking. This finding suggests that to create long-term changes in youth drinking and alcohol-related problems, strategies that change the environment should be used.

Despite the MLDA of 21, minors still have easy access to alcohol from commercial and social sources. The observed benefits of the MLDA have occurred with little or no active enforcement; simply by increasing enforcement levels and deterring adults from selling or providing alcohol to minors, even more injuries and deaths related to alcohol use among youth can be prevented each year.

Arguments for Lowering the Drinking Age Are Misguided

by the Center for Science in the Public Interest

About the author: *The Center for Science in the Public Interest is a nonprofit organization that promotes alcohol abuse prevention policies.*

> State Age-21 laws are one of the most effective public policies ever implemented in the Nation . . . I am chagrined to report that some supposedly responsible officials would like to repeal them.
>
> — Jim Hall, Chairman
> National Transportation Safety Board

Argument: Lowering the drinking age will reduce the allure of alcohol as a "forbidden fruit" for minors.

Response: Lowering the drinking age will make alcohol more available to an even younger population, replacing "forbidden fruit" with "low-hanging fruit."

The practices and behaviors of 18 year-olds are particularly influential on 15–17 year-olds. If 18 year-olds get the OK to drink, they will be modeling drinking for younger teens. Legal access to alcohol for 18 year-olds will provide more opportunities for younger teens to obtain it illegally from older peers.

Age-21 has resulted in decreases, not increases in youth drinking, an outcome inconsistent with an increased allure of alcohol. In 1983, one year before the National Minimum Purchase Age Act was passed, 88% of high school seniors reported any alcohol use in the past year and 41% reported binge drinking. By 1997, alcohol use by seniors had dropped to 75% and the percentage of binge drinkers had fallen to 31%.

Responsibility and Maturity

Argument: Lowering the drinking age will encourage young people to be responsible consumers. They'll get an idea of their tolerance and learn to drink

Reprinted, with permission, from "Talking Points/Arguments: Answering the Critics of Age-21," by the Center for Science in the Public Interest, February 1998, published at www.cspinet.org/booze/mlpatalk.htm. Reprinted with permission.

under supervision at bars (or on campus, if in college), rather than at uncontrolled private parties away from school.

Response: No evidence exists to indicate that kids will learn to drink responsibly simply because they are able to consume alcohol legally at a younger age. Countries with lower drinking ages suffer from alcohol-related problems similar to those in the U.S.

Responsible consumption comes with maturity, and maturity largely comes as certain protective mechanisms, such as marriage and first job, begin to take hold.

Supervision does not necessarily lead to responsibility. Many bars encourage irresponsible drinking by deeply discounting drinks and by heavily promoting specials, such as happy hours, two-for-ones, and bar crawls.

Raising the drinking age has apparently increased responsibility among young people. Compared to 1980 when less than 21 was the norm, fewer college students in 1995 reported drinking in the past month (68% vs. 82%) and binge drinking (39% vs. 44%). Also, more college students disapproved of binge drinking (66% vs. 57%).

The 1978 *National Study of Adolescent Drinking Behavior* found that 10th–12th graders in states with lower drinking ages drank significantly more, were drunk more often, and were less likely to abstain from alcohol. Additionally, national data

> *"Legal access to alcohol for 18 year-olds will provide more opportunities for younger teens to obtain it illegally from older peers."*

show that high school seniors who could not legally drink until age 21 drank less before age 21 and between ages 21–25 than did students in states with lower drinking ages.

Argument: At 18, kids can vote, join the military, sign contracts, and even smoke. Why shouldn't they be able to drink?

Response: Ages of initiation vary—One may vote at 18, drink at 21, rent a car at 25, and run for president at 35. These ages may appear arbitrary, but they take into account the requirements, risks, and benefits of each act.

When age-21 was challenged in Louisiana's State Supreme Court, the Court upheld the law, ruling that ". . . statutes establishing the minimum drinking age at a higher level than the age of majority are not arbitrary because they substantially further the appropriate governmental purpose of improving highway safety, and thus are constitutional."

Age-21 laws help keep kids healthy by postponing the onset of alcohol use. Deferred drinking reduces the risks of:

- developing alcohol dependence or abuse later in life.
- harming the developing brain.
- engaging in current and adult drug use.
- suffering alcohol-related problems, such as trouble at work, with friends, family, and police.

Stricter Enforcement Would Make Age-21 Laws More Effective

Argument: Minors still drink, so age-21 laws clearly don't work.

Response: Age-21 laws work. Young people drink less in response. The laws have saved an estimated 17,000 lives since states began implementing them in 1975, and they've decreased the number of alcohol-related youth fatalities among drivers by 63% since 1982.

Stricter enforcement of age-21 laws against commercial sellers would make those laws even more effective at reducing youth access to alcohol. The ease with which young people acquire alcohol—three-quarters of 8th graders say that it is "fairly easy" or "very easy" to get—indicates that more must be done. Current laws against sales to minors need stiff penalties to deter violations. Better education and prevention-oriented laws are needed to reduce the commercial pressures on kids to drink.

Lowering the drinking age in the past has sacrificed public health and safety:

- State motor vehicle fatality data from the 48 continental states found that lowering the drinking age for beer from 21 to 18 resulted in an 11% increase in fatalities among that age group.
- In Arizona, lowering the drinking age increased the incidence of fatal accidents by more than 25% and traffic fatalities by more than 35%.
- Lowering the drinking age in Massachusetts caused an increase in total fatal crashes, alcohol-related fatal crashes, and alcohol-related property damage crashes among 18–20 year-old drivers.
- From 1979–1984, the suicide rate was 9.7% greater among young people who could legally drink alcohol than among their peers who could not.

Raising the Drinking Age to 21 Has Been Counterproductive

by Ruth C. Engs

About the author: *Ruth C. Engs is a professor in the Department of Applied Health Sciences at Indiana University.*

The legal drinking age should be lowered to about 18 or 19 and young adults allowed to drink in controlled environments such as restaurants, taverns, pubs and official school and university functions. In these situations responsible drinking could be taught through role modeling and educational programs. Mature and sensible drinking behavior would be expected. This opinion is based upon research that I have been involved in for over twenty years concerning college age youth and the history of drinking in the United States and other cultures.

The Failure of Prohibition

Although the legal purchase age is 21 years of age, a majority of college students under this age consume alcohol but in an irresponsible manner. This is because drinking by these youth is seen as an enticing "forbidden fruit," a "badge of rebellion against authority" and a symbol of "adulthood." As a nation we have tried prohibition legislation twice in the past for controlling irresponsible drinking problems. This was during National Prohibition in the 1920s and state prohibition during the 1850s. These laws were finally repealed because they were unenforceable and because the backlash towards them caused other social problems. Today we are repeating history and making the same mistakes that occurred in the past. Prohibition did not work then and prohibition for young people under the age of 21 is not working now.

The flaunting of the current laws is readily seen among university students. Those under the age of 21 are more likely to be heavy—sometimes called "binge"—drinkers (consuming over 5 drinks at least once a week). For example, 22% of all students under 21 compared to 18% over 21 years of age are

Reprinted, with permission, from "Why the Drinking Age Should Be Lowered: An Opinion Based on Research," by Ruth C. Engs, published at www.indiana.edu/~engs/articles/cqoped.html. This article was adapted from and appeared within "Drinking on Campus," by Karen Scrivo, *CQ Researcher*, March 20, 1998.

heavy drinkers. Among drinkers only, 32% of under age compared to 24% of legal age are heavy drinkers.

Research from the early 1980s until the present has shown a continuous decrease in drinking and driving related variables which has paralleled the nation's, and also university students, decrease in per capita consumption. However, these declines started in 1980 before the national 1987 law which mandated states to have 21 year old alcohol purchase laws.

The decrease in drinking and driving problems is the result of many factors and not just the rise in purchase age or the decreased per capita consumption. These include: education concerning drunk driving, designated driver programs, increased seat belt and air bag usage, safer automobiles, lower speed limits, free taxi services from drinking establishments, etc.

An Increase in Alcohol Abuse

While there has been a decrease in per capita consumption and motor vehicle crashes, unfortunately, during this same time period there has been an *increase* in other problems related to heavy and irresponsible drinking among college age youth. Most of these reported behaviors showed little change until *after* the 21 year old law in 1987. For example from 1982 until 1987 about 46% of students reported "vomiting after drinking." This jumped to over 50% after the law change. Significant increases were also found for other variables: "cutting class after drinking" jumped from 9% to almost 12%; "missing class because of hangover" went from 26% to 28%; "getting lower grade because of drinking" rose from 5% to 7%; and "been in a fight after drinking" increased from 12% to 17%. All of these behaviors are indices of irresponsible drinking. This increase in abusive drinking behavior is due to "underground drinking" outside of adult supervision in student rooms and apartments where same age individuals congregate and because of lack of knowledge of responsible drinking behaviors.

Based upon the fact that our current prohibition laws are not working, the need for alternative approaches from the experience of other, and more ancient cultures, who do not have these problems need to be tried. Groups such as Italians, Greeks, Chinese and Jews, who have few drinking related problems, tend to share some common characteristics. Alcohol is neither seen as a poison or a magic potion, there is little or no social pressure to drink, irresponsible behavior is never tolerated, young people learn at home from their parents and from other adults how to handle alcohol in a responsible manner, there is societal consensus on what constitutes responsible drinking. Because the 21 year old drinking age law is not working, and is counterproductive, it behooves us as a nation to change our current prohibition law and to teach responsible drinking techniques for those who choose to consume alcoholic beverages.

The Drinking Age Should Be Lowered to 18

by Michael Clay Smith

About the author: *Michael Clay Smith is a professor of criminal justice at the University of Southern Mississippi.*

In the 1980s, in an ebullient bid to curtail drunk driving by teenagers, the government imposed a nationwide minimum drinking age of 21. It was a kind of second Prohibition, albeit for young adults only. The law's goal, of course, was to make young people happier, healthier, and safer.

By now it is obvious that the law has not succeeded in preventing the under-21 group from drinking. The popular press and higher-education media are filled with reports of high-visibility, alcohol-related troubles on our campuses. Serious riots by students who want to do their boozing unhindered have broken out at many institutions. Some of the melees, such as those at Ohio University, the University of Colorado, and Pennsylvania State University, have involved significant injuries and many arrests.

The Failure of Age-21 Laws

Reports of binge drinking come from all types of campuses across the country. In 1992, researchers reported that more college students were drinking to get drunk than their counterparts a decade earlier, and one recent study reported an increase, just since 1994, in the number of students who drink deliberately to get drunk. Of particular pertinence, in another national study, Ruth Engs and Beth Diebold of Indiana University and David Hanson of the State University of New York at Potsdam reported in 1996 in the *Journal of Alcohol and Drug Education* that, compared with those of legal age, a significantly higher percentage of students under age 21 were heavy drinkers.

Worst of all are the reports of drinking-related deaths. In 1997, at least two fraternity pledges died of alcohol poisoning, and in 1995 a third choked to death on his own vomit, all after initiation-night parties. One informal survey

Reprinted, with permission, from "Treat Students as Adults: Set the Drinking Age at 18, Not 21," by Michael Clay Smith, *Chronicle of Higher Education*, March 12, 1999.

of alcohol-related deaths among college students during 1997 turned up 11 more fatalities: Three students fell from dormitory windows, one darted into the path of a motorcycle, one fell through a greenhouse roof, another was asphyxiated, and five died in highway crashes. At Frostburg State University, seven students were charged with manslaughter in 1997 in connection with the death of a freshman who guzzled beer and 12 to 14 shots of vodka in two hours at a fraternity party.

America's second experiment with Prohibition seems to have been no more effective than the first one. In fact, we suspect that setting the drinking age at 21 is itself one cause of our present alcohol problems. While other factors may be at work, too, giving liquor the status of contraband seems to have invested it with a mystique, rendering its use- and abuse-chic and even de rigueur, especially in fraternity and sorority life.

> *"For most other purposes today, we treat 18-year-olds as adults. . . . It is blatantly inconsistent to forbid them to drink."*

For most other purposes today, we treat 18-year-olds as adults. They can vote for President, fire a rifle for the military, buy and sell real estate, and raise families of their own. It is blatantly inconsistent to forbid them to drink. Many of them view the setting of the drinking age at 21 as hypocritical. Small wonder it hasn't worked.

The Harms of Age-21 Laws for College Students

It is indisputable that a drinking age of 21 has had harmful effects on campus life:

• It has soured relations between students and police. As usual, when police officers must enforce an unpopular law, acrimony grows between those who do the enforcing and those who are the targets of the enforcement. Such bad feeling has negative effects of its own: It undermines students' rapport with police officers at a time when crime rates are high, and it has the potential to create in students a life-long animosity toward police in general—not a healthy attitude in a democracy.

• It has left otherwise promising students with police records. Charges of underage possession—and the charges of public intoxication and disorderly conduct that often accompany them—will in many cases stay on a person's record for a lifetime. And students over 21 who, as commonly happens, party with friends a few years younger get rap sheets for giving alcohol to minors. A record of that sort could prove to be a problem when the time comes to look for a job, apply for a professional license, or seek admission to graduate school. What's more, people with police records, even relatively minor ones, sometimes begin to see themselves as flawed, mavericks, or even outlaws—criminologists call this phenomenon "labeling." These are heavy prices to pay for young people whose only sin was to engage in the traditional campus rituals of beer drinking and partying.

• The higher drinking age has curtailed faculty members' engagement with students. Professors used to involve themselves in the development of the whole student, serving as advisers to clubs or fraternities and sororities, and sometimes entertaining students in their homes. Now, however, many faculty members are afraid to meet students in a social setting because of the threat of criminal and civil liability that hangs over an adult who, even unknowingly, is present when people under 21 drink.

• The drinking age of 21 has driven student partying to less public and thus more dangerous, venues. To avoid being caught drinking illegally, students frequently party off campus. With less oversight from adults, heavy drinking, brawling, and sexual misconduct are more likely to occur.

Getting Tougher May Not Be the Answer

[Since 1997] Americans have seen a hardening of prohibition efforts, with so-called "zero tolerance" enforcement on many campuses. Yet many observers feel that the problem is worsening, even as administrators become stricter. Could it be that getting tougher has been the wrong strategy, doomed because it flies in the face of nature? We now know that many college students will continue to drink, no matter what the consequences.

Many factors have contributed to colleges' present difficulties. Lowering the drinking age would not be a panacea. Yet it would unquestionably eliminate many small- and even medium-aggravations among students, police officers, and administrators. It would allow enforcement and intervention efforts to be redirected from pesky matters such as minors' possession of alcohol to the authentic dangers—pernicious inebriation and drunken driving. It would bring the drinking laws into congruence with the fact that legal adulthood in the United States today begins at age 18. It's worth a try.

Chapter 5

What Measures Are Effective in Reducing Teen Alcohol Abuse?

Chapter Preface

Many people believe that the most effective way to reduce teen alcohol abuse is to reduce teen access to alcohol. Surveys of high school students find that the majority of teens who drink obtain their alcohol from adults. Teens may pay adult strangers or friends who are over age twenty-one to buy alcohol for them.

Many parents also provide their teenage children with alcohol, a practice that is legal in all fifty states. But some parents also host parties—often after high school graduation—where alcohol is served, allowing their teenager's friends to drink as well. In many communities this had led to conflicts among parents, many of whom believe that providing alcohol to teenagers is dangerous and irresponsible.

Some communities and states have responded by passing social host liability laws. Under these laws, adults who serve or provide alcohol to persons under the age of twenty-one can be held liable if an underage person who was given alcohol is killed or injured, or kills or injures another person. In Minnesota those convicted under the state's Zero Adult Providers law can be jailed, fined, or sued for damages. According to the University of Minnesota Alcohol Epidemiology Program, "Social host liability laws send a clear message to adults that providing alcohol to underage youth is not acceptable." In North Carolina, anyone convicted of providing alcohol to underage persons is fined a minimum of $250 and assigned twenty-five hours of community service, and in Maryland, adult providers can be charged up to $1,000 for a first offense. Jon Mattleman, the director of a youth commission in suburban Boston, believes that "letting parents know that they put themselves at risk will have an impact."

Social host liability laws have not been passed in most communities because they are resisted by many parents and are difficult to enforce. Keg registration laws have been a more popular alternative. These laws make it easier for police to identify the purchasers of kegs confiscated at parties where underage youth have consumed alcohol.

Targeting the adults who provide alcohol to those under twenty-one is one way to reduce teen access to alcohol. The viewpoints in this chapter explore other measures that aim to reduce drunk driving, binge drinking, and other forms of alcohol abuse among teens.

Banning Sales of Alcohol over the Internet Would Reduce Underage Drinking

by Americans for Responsible Alcohol Access

About the author: Americans for Responsible Alcohol Access is a coalition established to prevent illegal shipment of alcoholic beverages and to discourage underage access to these products.

In 1998 and 1999, at least three dozen television stations in major cities around the country did investigative reports to test ARAA's argument that illegal alcohol shipments that follow some Internet sales create a new and incredibly easy way for teenagers to acquire beer, wine, and liquor. Every one of them documented what some representing the California wine industry continue to deny—it is literally child's play for today's cyber-savvy young people to order alcohol over the Internet or by toll-free phone and have it delivered to their homes or college dormitories, no questions asked.

A Pandora's Box to Underage Access

Most Americans agree that direct illegal shipping is a Pandora's Box to underage access. It's no secret that today's teenagers are savvy when it comes to acquiring alcohol. And unregulated direct shipments of alcohol to customers is an open invitation for youngsters to log on to the Internet, download "cyberliquor" or order via toll-free calls that don't show up on their parents' phone bill. A recent poll confirmed that most Americans believe this is a bad idea—85 percent believe "the sale of alcohol over the Internet or through the mail should not be allowed because it would give minors easier access to alcohol and could result in more abuse."

At a time when alcohol-related teen highway fatalities are on the rise, we should not be making it easier for them to buy alcohol. Ironically, direct shipping advocates say that concern about underage access to alcohol is a "red herring." Stings conducted by state officials from Colorado to New York prove that teens can readily obtain alcohol through the Internet and other direct shipping schemes. The facts point not to a "red herring," but should be a red flag for the public:

- Youth (ages 15–20) alcohol-related traffic fatalities increased by almost 5 percent in 1999. (source: National Highway Traffic Safety Administratioin.)
- This increase bucks the overall alcohol trends: Alcohol-related traffic fatalities have been declining for many years among the general population and even among teens (down 50% over the past decade). There can be only one reason why alcohol-related teen traffic fatalities were up in 1999—more teens are getting access to alcohol and driving.
- In 1999, 2,238 teens (15–20) were killed in alcohol-related crashes.
- In future years, demographics will place more teens at risk: By 2005, the youth population is expected to increase by 14 percent.

Direct Shipping Removes Safeguards to Underage Access

With illegal direct shipping, teens don't have to worry about risks associated with purchasing from local outlets. No longer do they have to forge fake ID's and chance getting caught and arrested for buying alcohol at a store monitored by the police. All they have to do is dial a toll-free number or log on the Internet and mouse-click "Yes" to the question of whether they are of age. They can pay by credit card or even the new checking account debit cards which function much the same as a credit card. Indeed, most students go off to college these days with a credit card, yet most are not of legal drinking age until their junior year. Delivery truck drivers are not in the business of checking ID's—and in any case many direct shippers don't label their packages or [they] intentionally list contents deceptively.

Every state has set age 21 as the legal drinking age. This unity was intended to save lives by eliminating the former situation in the U.S. in which states had differing legal drinking ages. This created "blood borders" across which underage drinkers would drive to get access to alcohol. Passage of "21" laws in all states effectively eliminated the "blood borders." But Internet and toll-free direct shipment creates a new, technological blood border that touches every state.

The Internet was supposed to be an information superhighway . . . a detour around state and local regulations that encourage responsible control and usage of alcohol. Illegal shippers say that kids cannot order

> *"85 percent [of Americans] believe 'the sale of alcohol over the Internet or through the mail should not be allowed.'"*

alcohol on the Internet, but that's what was said about pornography. The truth is, you can get whatever you want on the Internet . . . without restriction. The Internet cannot verify age . . . and delivery truck drivers are not in the business of "carding" the recipients of packages they deliver.

Most Americans don't regard beer, wine, and liquor in the same manner as other consumer products and don't think it should be sold in the same way. But those lobbying to legalize direct alcohol shipment to customers argue that ordering wine, beer, and liquor should be no different than ordering a garment from a clothing catalogue. A national Wirthlin survey confirmed that they're out of step with most of America: Four out of five respondents believe "the sale and shipment of beer, wine, or liquor over the Internet or through the mail directly to consumers should not be allowed." Large majorities support the current state licensed distribution system because, while not perfect, it does a relatively effective job of responsibly regulating alcohol and discouraging access to minors.

Direct Shippers Deliberately Confuse the Issue with False Arguments

Supporters of direct shipping to consumers argue that kids aren't going to be ordering $60 bottles of Chardonnay. That's true, but it's a false argument. Obviously, teenagers aren't going to order fine wine. Instead, they order lower-priced beer, wine, and liquor which also are available by direct shipment. Whether a $60 bottle or $4 bottle it's all ordered the same way and delivered the same way—right to the doorstep, often during after-school hours when parents are working. No wonder 85 percent of the American people oppose these illegal shipments because they know it makes it easier for underage access and abuse.

"Reform" and "compromise" proposals pushed by the direct shipping lobby are fundamentally flawed because they rely on an honor system which cannot prevent shipments to minors and to "dry" counties around the country. State agencies have neither the resources nor the authority to ensure that all shipped packages that might contain alcoholic beverages are not delivered to minors.

Consumers in most states already are able to legally obtain brands not regularly available at their local outlets. Small producers have available to them legal Internet-based marketing and distribution outlets such as evineyard to get their brands to consumers through the existing state systems. Also, wholesalers and retailers are willing to represent any of the brands of small producers that are being shipped illegally to consumers. But many direct-shippers are deliberately not cooperating because their goal is to dismantle the states' licensed alcohol control system.

The Government Should Not Ban Internet Alcohol Sales

by the *Atlanta Journal-Constitution*

About the author: *The* Atlanta Journal-Constitution, *a major regional newspaper, ran the following editorial while Congress was considering legislation that would grant state attorneys general the power to go to federal court to block direct shipments of alcoholic beverages from producers to consumers. The 21st Amendment Enforcement Act became law in 2000.*

Liquor distributors are doing evil. They're pushing legislation in Congress that could block direct sales from producers to consumers. The problem, they say, is that out-of-control teens are buying beer and wine by phone or over the Internet with parents' credit cards.

Restricting Competition

What lawmakers are promoting now is restricted competition of legal commerce. In a turf war where wineries are seeking market access and distributors are intoxicated by their monopoly, consumers are the losers. Consider the profits in an industry where annual wine sales are $17 billion, beer generates $174.9 billion and distilled spirits $89 billion. Where the top distributor, with 11.8 percent of the market, will earn revenue of $2.82 billion [in 1999]. Where sales and excise taxes are in the billions. (In Georgia, excise taxes range from $2.28 for a case of beer to $14.64 for a case of liquor.) And where direct sales of wine, a mere $500 million now, will surge as Americans' Internet comfort level grows.

The distributors, a powerful Washington lobby, have managed to get the support of 21 state attorneys general with this claim.

U.S. Representative Joe Scarborough (R-Fla.), the bill's chief sponsor, says the legislation "is a great first step in helping parents keep illegal alcohol out of their children's hands . . .The Internet will no longer be a bootlegger's paradise."

Few Teenagers Have Access

Exactly how many teenagers have access to their parents' credit cards, are willing to risk using them, wait patiently for the shipment to be sent and hope that nobody's home when the shipment arrives?

While this scenario may work in a dramatic sting operation, in real life this is rare. Certainly, it isn't frequent enough to warrant federal intervention. California, which has allowed wine shipments to its residents for 36 years, investigates 10,000 complaints a year of minors trying to buy alcohol. Only one has involved an Internet attempt.

The liquor distributors are a legacy of the post-Prohibition era when, amid fear of organized crime's takeover, states mandated a three-tier system—manufacturer to wholesaler/distributor to retailer—and barred investment in more than one tier. In the 1960s, more than 10,000 wholesalers distributed liquor. Today, through consolidation, there are about 300. The top five own about about a third of the market.

"For many small wineries . . . direct sales is their only means of survival."

And then, as now, they're protected by their very own constitutional amendment: the 21st, passed in 1933 to make the repeal of Prohibition more palatable. It bars "the transportation into any state . . . of intoxicating liquors, in violation of the laws thereof." A state ban on importation of any other legal product would violate the Constitution's commerce clause, which forbids states to restrict interstate commerce. Yet in Georgia, Florida, Kentucky, Maryland and Tennessee, it's a felony to ship liquor to residents.

Small Businesses Will Suffer

Meanwhile, distribution charges for alcohol are the highest of any packaged-goods industry and twice as much as food distribution, meaning higher consumer prices. For many small wineries unable to afford the distributors' costs or too small to get the shelf space, direct sales is their only means of survival.

Colleges Must Use a Variety of Strategies to Reduce Alcohol Abuse on Campus

by Henry Wechsler

About the author: *Henry Wechsler is director of the Harvard School of Public Health College Alcohol Study, an ongoing survey of 15,000 students at 140 four-year colleges in 40 states.*

Since results from our first survey were published [in 1994], heavy episodic alcohol use or "binge drinking" among college students has become a nationally recognized problem. Seventy percent of college presidents consider binge drinking a problem for their institutions, but they don't know how to counteract it. This is no surprise, since there has not, up to now, been sufficient, scientifically credible information about what is effective. Some approaches seem promising, but they usually have been evaluated on a single campus only, often without control groups.

In this article, we are now able to offer selected findings from our College Alcohol Study (CAS) that can be used to shape intervention campaigns to address the problem of binge drinking. Since 1993, over 50,000 students in a nationally representative sample of 140 colleges in 39 states have responded to our three surveys. We've asked questions about alcohol use and abuse, experience with prevention programs, encounters with enforcement or control policies, and attitudes toward school initiatives. We've learned a number of important lessons to guide college responses to student alcohol abuse.

Colleges Must Act

There is general agreement today about the nature of the problem. The CAS national findings clearly demonstrate that binge drinking is prevalent on most college campuses. Nationally, two in five students binge drink—defined as consuming five or more drinks in a row for men and four for women—at least once in a two-week period. These students experience a higher rate of various educational, social, and health problems than their non-binging peers. Half of the students who binge drink do so more than once a week. Half of these frequent binge drinkers report having five or more different alcohol-related problems during the school year. This rate is 20 times greater than that for students who drink but do not binge.

Beyond the harm they cause for themselves, binge drinkers affect others on campus. Non-binging students who attend schools in which more than half of the students binge drink are more than twice as likely to report such second-hand effects as insults and arguments, vandalism, physical assaults, or unwanted sexual advances than are students in schools with fewer binge drinkers.

> *"Colleges must protect their students from [the] negative effects of alcohol."*

At most campuses, these problems are just too severe to ignore. While deaths are relatively rare, most large colleges report numerous overdoses—admissions for acute alcoholic poisonings—in their student health centers or community emergency rooms. In our survey, 0.6 percent of students report needing treatment for alcohol overdose. While this seems like a small number, projected nationally it could add up to over 30,000 students a year. Each year, one in eight students reports injuries resulting from alcohol use, and one in 20 reports injuries severe enough to require medical treatment.

Binge drinking also affects students' academic performance, with half of binge drinkers reporting that they missed at least one class as a result of their alcohol use, and more than a third saying they fell behind in their schoolwork due to drinking. Binge drinkers are also more likely to report lower grades than non-bingers.

Colleges must protect their students from these negative effects of alcohol. One in eight non-binge-drinking students nationwide reported being assaulted physically or having personal property vandalized due to another student's alcohol use. The everyday effects of binge drinking disrupt the process of higher education. Taking care of drunks, having sleep and study disturbed, and worrying about one's physical safety are incompatible with the atmosphere required for optimal learning to take place.

One Size Does Not Fit All

Binge drinking rates at different colleges range from one to 80 percent of students. This variation suggests that institutional approaches should be shaped by the particular conditions of a given campus. Many factors—the attitudes and experiences students bring to school, social and institutional features of the college, and characteristics of the adjoining community—contribute to student alcohol problems. Colleges vary with respect to each of these factors, including for example, the levels of drinking during high school by their incoming freshmen, the size and status of their fraternities and sororities, and the number and political strength of local alcohol outlets. The response of colleges must take these variations into account; there are no "one-size-fits-all" solutions. While we here offer national statistics that can be used in shaping campaigns, each college needs to take stock of its own particular situation. A comprehensive self-diagnosis is the necessary first step.

Alcohol Education Is Not Enough

A natural response for colleges wishing to address binge drinking is to educate students about the problems of alcohol use. Results from our surveys of college administrators indicate that curriculum infusion, dedicated classes, and poster or communications campaigns are a regular part of most school efforts. Student reports reflect this educational emphasis. Four of five students have been exposed to some alcohol education effort. Two of three students have seen posters or signs and report having read announcements or articles.

The problem, however, is that most of the heaviest drinkers too easily ignore all this; indeed, they do not view their drinking as a problem. Only one-quarter of the frequent binge drinkers say they ever had a drinking problem; two of three students who drink that way consider themselves "moderate drinkers."

While education is needed, by itself it will not solve the problem. Binge drinkers, in fact, are more likely than non-binge drinkers to report they have received information from the school. Moreover, the most at-risk groups on campus—members of Greek organizations and athletes—are already targeted for educational interventions in an over-whelming majority of survey schools. Eighty percent of schools report offering special educational programs for athletes, while two-thirds offer programs for fraternity members and 60 percent for sorority members.

In other words, college students have been told about the risks of alcohol use, yet they continue to binge drink. While our evidence demonstrates that schools are targeting the right audiences for their interventions, it suggests that the impact is limited. Reliance solely on educational interventions to reduce alcohol use is an inadequate response. Colleges need to move beyond a simple didactic model.

Student Support for Tougher Policies

Many colleges are considering an increase in controls over alcohol; pressures to do so have risen in the wake of a number of highly visible deaths on college campuses in the past two years. Administrators are caught between the fear that a tragic event will occur if they don't tighten controls over alcohol and the threat of student protests and potential riots if they do. While our results indicate that colleges that ban alcohol for everyone on campus—including of-age students—

have lower rates of binge drinking and associated problems, the causal direction of this relationship is not clear. It may be that it is easier to ban alcohol at colleges with low binge rates, or that a third factor—such as a shared concern among students and administrators over the negative effects of heavy drinking—is responsible for both the lower rates and the strict policy.

"While education is needed, by itself it will not solve the problem."

When considering whether to adopt tougher control measures, it should not be a foregone conclusion that students will strongly oppose such a change. Some will, as the still vivid memories of students throwing debris at police or burning furniture in protest suggest. However, our data indicate that many students are concerned about the role alcohol plays in their life at college. Half of all students nationally believe that alcohol is a problem on their campus; considerable support exists for a wide array of possible policy controls. Among colleges that strengthened their alcohol policies between 1993 and 1997, nearly one-quarter did so in response to pressure from students.

College administrators should realize that they have a lot more support to implement policy changes than they think they do. Although this may come as a surprise to administrators confronted by angry students demanding the "right" to drink as much as they want, more than half of all students nationally favor more college intervention. There is considerable student support for a wide array of possible policy controls that may help impact binge drinking and related harms.

Marginalizing the Heaviest Drinkers

Frequent binge drinkers are out of touch with the way alcohol problems are perceived by others on campus. Only one in five students engages in this type of drinking, yet this group accounts for two-thirds of all the alcohol consumed by college students; more than half of all the alcohol-related problems students experience; and over 60 percent of all the reported injuries, vandalism, and problems with the police.

While most of these students don't think they have a problem with alcohol, their schools have a problem with them. Frequent binge drinkers oppose efforts by college administrators to reduce levels of problem drinking and related harms. These are the students most likely to protest, not always peacefully, in support of the item most important to them: beer. But in this stance, they are out of step with most other students, even the occasional binge drinkers. . . .

Administrators and students need to appreciate that the heaviest drinkers are a vocal, highly visible, but relatively small minority. Up to now, given peer pressure to drink, non-bingers have often felt marginalized, with the best they could ask for being separate, alcohol-free dorms. The segregation should work the other way, with students who disturb the peace moved to dorms for people whose behaviors indicate they need extra supervision.

When students are looking for social activities, few alternatives can compete with the low cost of alcohol. A recent survey of bars and retail liquor outlets in 10 college communities makes this point very clearly.

Social activities that involve alcohol appeal to students on a cost basis. Alcohol is cheap, plentiful, and easy to get. For the price of one movie ticket (not including concessions), a student could buy eight drinks at a bar, 15 cans of beer, or entrance for three people to an "all-you-can-drink-party." On all of these campuses, students can find a way to binge drink for less than five dollars. Students who pay less than a dollar per drink, or who pay a set fee for "all-you-can-drink," are more likely to drink at binge levels than students who have to pay more. Econometric analyses of alcohol use have shown that price does play a role in binge drinking, particularly among women.

A high density of alcohol outlets surrounds most larger campuses. Establishments cater to college students and compete with each other to draw business. Frequently this competition translates into price wars: local outlets undercut each other and make up the difference by selling large volumes. College communities can examine the distribution of liquor outlets and the pricing practices in the neighborhoods around them. They can then begin a process of dialogue and concerted action with community leaders to solve these problems.

Designated Helpers

College students are motivated by positive messages that align with their values. They tend to be less responsive to rule-based approaches than to positive visions of their role. Indeed, social factors—like the number of close friends and hours spent socializing with friends—are important predictors of binge drinking, independent of age, religion, personal and family alcohol history, and other substance use.

One norm among students that can be a very powerful motivator is their desire to see that their friends are safe. Half of students nationally report that they have taken care of another student who was drunk, an important indicator of student values. Positive messages can capitalize on these existing motivations and reinforce safe behaviors.

"Colleges that ban alcohol for everyone on campus—including of-age students—have lower rates of binge drinking."

Anti-drunk-driving campaigns have profited from similar messages promoting informal controls of drinking behavior among friends. This approach may hold even more promise for college students: messages can appeal to their desire to protect their friends. "Friends don't let friends drive drunk" is a message that resonates with a highly social group. Similar messages aimed at students can enhance peer support for discouraging others from getting drunk, acting irresponsibly, having sex when they are drunk, or burdening their friends with unsafe behavior. "Friends don't let friends lose control" may be an appropriate message for students who fear the secondhand effects of alcohol or the increasingly litigious repercussions of going out or hooking up while under the influence.

Another message that can resonate is that in group situations, some students owe it to others to abstain. In some of the recent, highly publicized overdose deaths, the people who were taking care of the student who died were also intoxicated and unable to recognize the seriousness of the situation.

A Women's Health Issue

Women are affected at lower dosage levels of alcohol than men. In our survey, we employed a gender-specific measure of binge drinking to account for the greater number of problems women experience at the same consumption rate as men. Women who join sororities have had fewer binge-drinking experiences in high school than men who join fraternities, yet in college they binge drink at the same rate as men. The mix of alcohol and inexperience puts them in grave jeopardy for sexual assault. Acquaintance rape is one of the most salient health issues for women on college campuses. Nationally, one of 10 female frequent binge drinkers reported engaging in non-consensual sex while under the influence of alcohol.

> *"One norm among students that can be a very powerful motivator is their desire to see that their friends are safe."*

Female students are an important target group for promoting mutual caretaking messages. Informally today we already see women designated to stay sober and watch out for their friends at heavy drinking parties.

Many college campuses have well-established women's centers that are credible and effective advocates for women's health and status. The staff of these centers need to be concerned about the ways in which binge drinking and alcohol abuse are women's health issues. Women's centers on colleges should be partners in efforts to reduce binge drinking and related harms.

Enablers May Disable

It is especially important to pay attention to mutual caretaking motives in light of the evidence on how underage students obtain alcohol.

A great deal of collegiate energy and prevention resources are spent on combating fake IDs. Yet this technique for obtaining alcohol is used by only one in five underage students. How do they get alcohol? Four of five underage drinkers get their alcohol from older students. One-third of older students have been asked by underage students to provide them with alcohol, and almost all complied. This is one student norm that needs to be challenged!

Of-age students view providing alcohol to minors as a gesture of friendship and don't consider the potential for harm. To them, this form of sharing is a positive act. We need to make a clear distinction for these students between positive and negative acts of "sharing" alcohol. What kind of "friendship" would enable heavy drinking?

Student Rights

While we hear from students demanding a right to drink, there have been few public demonstrations for a binge-free college environment. According to our data, most college students have experienced secondhand effects of binge drinking, but few complain about it. Seven in eight non-binge-drinking students have been affected negatively by the drinking of others, yet only one of seven students living in dormitories reports having complained to a resident advisor about other students' drinking. Students may choose not to complain due to social pressure or fear of retaliation.

The change needed is for all students to understand that they have far more fundamental rights as students than any claimed "right" of a few to drink. The rights of all students to live and learn in a habitable dormitory environment need to be reestablished as a part of college policy addressing binge drinking. A campaign that informs students of their basic right to a quality of campus life free from the secondhand effects of binge drinking is needed. Agreement with student governments about unacceptable behavior in a group living situation, and enforcement of the resulting code of conduct, is an important step toward reducing the harms of excessive alcohol use.

Students almost universally support alcohol-free living environments. Nearly nine out of every 10 students support a policy by colleges that would provide alcohol-free dormitories on campus. Some have voted already with their feet. Eighteen percent of students report that they already live in an alcohol-free dorm; 24 percent more say they would like to live in one. Altogether, three of five non-bingers either live in—or want to live in—an alcohol-free dorm.

> *"Women's centers on college campuses should be partners in efforts to reduce binge drinking."*

Binge drinking is the most serious problem affecting social life, health, and education on college campuses today. Colleges should develop campaigns specifically tailored for their campuses, using our survey data as a start, and using what they know about local problems and resources. On a national level, our overall recommendations point to issues that deserve attention. These issues lend themselves to local campaigns undertaken by college administrators, communications experts, and prevention specialists.

The Goal of Eliminating Drinking on College Campuses Is Unrealistic

by Edward H. Hammond

About the author: *Edward H. Hammond is president of Fort Hayes State University and served as chairman of the National Collegiate Alcohol Awareness Week in October 1997.*

The recent deaths of college students in Louisiana, Massachusetts, and Virginia from consuming too much alcohol are paramount tragedies which we should all work to prevent. But if we draw the wrong lessons from these deaths, they will occur again and again.

Most Students Are Responsible

We live in a complex society, and perhaps no portion of our society is more complex than a college or university campus. In a five-minute stroll across campus, a casual observer can find students who are undergoing a rite of passage into adulthood, others who are doggedly hanging on to prerogatives of adolescence, and still others who are well along in developing the key life skills of good judgment, self-discipline, and mature, responsible decision making. The good news is that the vast majority of students fall into this last category.

Let's start with some basic facts drawn from a recent study conducted by the Core Institute at Southern Illinois University. At least two-thirds of college students say they don't binge drink, 72 percent have never missed a class because of drinking, and 67 percent say they do not drive under the influence of alcohol. Although these statistics are not cause for complacency or inactivity regarding alcohol consumption among college students, they do paint a more realistic picture of a problem which needs to be solved and thus increase our ability to find a workable strategy.

The fact is, the drinking age splits the college population. Students who are

Reprinted from "Whitewashing Fences and Campus Alcohol Prohibition," by Edward H. Hammond, *Black Issues in Higher Education*, January 8, 1998, by permission of *Black Issues in Higher Education*.

twenty-one and older can purchase alcohol legally and, according to the U.S. Census Bureau, account for nearly 70 percent of the college population. In an era when many high school seniors take a year or two off between graduation and their freshman year at college, at a time in which a considerable percentage of all students spend more than the traditional four years as undergrads, and in a job market that requires advanced degrees for an increasing number of entry-level positions, simple rules that try to ban alcohol from college campuses don't work.

Alcohol Policies Must Be Realistic

That's why these alcohol-related tragedies must be viewed in a broader, more realistic context. Rather than giving in to the obvious, understandable—but mistaken—notion that the proper response to these deaths is to limit access to alcohol for all students, we need to recognize that such a strategy could backfire. Instead of spending all of our attention and energy on prohibition, we need to understand that—like Tom Sawyer whitewashing Aunt Polly's fence—such a simplistic approach may make an undesirable thing look very desirable indeed, thereby promoting just the kind of behavior we'd like to discourage.

Now let's apply the insights of researchers to this problem. Many of those who have studied drinking among college students—such as Dr. Michael Haines of Northern Illinois University—have noted that distortions of what is really happening on campus have the effect of "normalizing the misbehavior we are trying to prevent."

In other words, if students—for whatever reason—perceive a particular type of behavior to be the norm, groups of students are likely to alter their personal actions to fit in with the crowd. Thus, by focusing our attention on the problem of binge drinking—a type of behavior that characterizes a minority of the campus population—it is possible that we are helping to create a "false norm" that encourages precisely the type of behavior we are trying to eliminate.

> *"Simple rules that try to ban alcohol from college campuses don't work."*

We may be saying, "Binge drinking is a terrible and dangerous problem. Don't do it!" But at least some kids will hear, "Binge drinking is what most people do when they're in college, but you should be different."

Changing Attitudes

As chairman of National College Alcohol Awareness Week, which was in October [1997], I know that it is more productive to focus on changing attitudes that will ultimately lead to changes in behavior. We need to make sure that students know that the majority rules—and that the majority believes in and practices good judgment, self-discipline, and mature, responsible decision making. And the most effective way to spread that behavior is through peer-to-peer education that combines positive peer pressure with information on alcohol and its effects.

Let me be very clear. For the 30 percent of students who are under the legal drinking age, our message should be straightforward: "Don't break the law because not only is underage drinking illegal, it's dangerous!" For all students, our message about binge drinking should be equally straightforward: "Binge drinking is dangerous to your health and can be deadly. Don't do it!"

But for those who can purchase alcohol legally, we should give them realistic advice: "As an adult, you can choose to drink. If you do drink, remember that the majority rules and do so responsibly."

By understanding the complexity of a college campus, and by recognizing that a large percentage of the students at most colleges and universities can drink legally if they choose to, we can reinforce the healthy norm. By spotlighting and drawing attention to the number of legal drinkers who drink responsibly, we can help create a standard of behavior that will change attitudes and actions in a positive and non-destructive way.

Zero-Tolerance Laws Are Effective in Reducing Drunk Driving Among Youth

by Robert Shearouse

About the author: *Robert Shearouse is the national director of public policy for Mothers Against Drunk Driving.*

The 21-year-old minimum drinking age has been the law nationwide since 1986. Several states actually adopted "21" laws before that time and it's estimated that such laws have saved more than 16,500 lives since 1975.

But until recently, it wasn't against the law in many states for drivers under 21 to drink and drive. This conduct wasn't deemed illegal for young drivers until their blood alcohol content (BAC) exceeded the illegal drunk driving limit established by each state for all drivers—either .08 or .10 percent BAC.

Zero Tolerance Saves Lives

In 1995, Congress passed legislation requiring all states to adopt "zero tolerance" laws for drivers under 21 by the year 1999. Zero tolerance laws make it illegal for people under 21 to drive with any measurable amount (maximum of 0.02 BAC) of alcohol in their bodies because it's illegal for them to drink in the first place. In the spring of 1998, South Carolina became the 50th state to adopt zero tolerance.

Zero tolerance saves young lives. Maryland's zero tolerance law produced an 11 percent decrease in drinking drivers under 21 involved in crashes. Another study showed that 12 states with zero tolerance laws experienced a 16 percent decrease in single-vehicle, nighttime fatal crashes compared to states without zero tolerance.

Despite these facts, the youth death toll from alcohol-related traffic crashes is still high. In 1997, 6,258 people, ages 15–20, were killed in traffic crashes and 2,209 of these deaths—more than 35 percent—involved alcohol. Young people

From "Zero Tolerance for Young Drivers: It's the Law, but Is It Being Enforced?" by Robert Shearouse, *Driven*, Fall 1998. Reprinted by permission of Mothers Against Drunk Driving.

are over-represented in alcohol-related fatal crashes. The alcohol involvement fatal crash rate for young drivers is about twice that of drivers over 21. Are we achieving the maximum benefits from zero tolerance laws and, if not, why? Research on California's zero tolerance law is telling. It showed a marginal effect on the number of youthful drivers in fatal crashes; reduction in the number of DUI charges against minors to zero tolerance citations; a slight increase in overall drinking and driving actions against youth; and no increase in young peoples' awareness of the law nor perception of arrest risk.

Lax Enforcement

Many states aren't realizing the full lifesaving benefits of zero tolerance because the effectiveness of these laws is watered down. The reasons are inadequate enforcement, failure of courts to treat these offenses seriously, lack of public awareness of the law and ignorance of zero tolerance's potential benefits for all these groups.

We must do a better job of educating the public that zero tolerance laws exist and they save lives when enforced stringently. Equally as important, law enforcement officers, judges and all participants in the criminal justice system must recognize the lifesaving benefits of zero tolerance. This recognition inevitably will lead to strict enforcement and meaningful adjudication.

Now, some law enforcement officers are reluctant to arrest young people and give them a criminal record, or subject them to license suspension "just" because they may have had only "one beer." Processing juveniles also can be time-consuming since these offenders generally cannot be whisked off to jail— they often must be held until their parents pick them up or they get processed through juvenile facilities. Police feel that zero tolerance laws make them into "baby-sitters." The perceived risk of apprehension is low among young drivers and the general deterrent effect of the law is lost. Often, the court gives these youthful offenders a "break" or treats their offenses as non-moving, non-alcohol-related offenses. Law enforcement officers are going to be even more reluctant to enforce the laws if they know that judges aren't going to take them seriously. Imagine what young people must think: they know the courts frequently don't view this as a serious offense and even if they are arrested, they won't suffer serious consequences.

Communities Must Work to Make Zero Tolerance a Reality

The effectiveness of laws depends on strict enforcement, vigorous prosecution and meaningful disposition. If police and court officials aren't fully enforcing and applying zero tolerance, local citizens must demand it. Elected officials must be held accountable for public safety and that includes the safety of our youth.

Communities must work to make zero tolerance a reality—not just another law on the books. For more information, contact the MADD National Programs Department at (214) 744-6233.

Recognizing False IDs Can Help Reduce Underage Drinking

by Roger Johnson

About the author: *FBI Special Agent Roger Johnson serves as the assistant section chief for the Alcohol and Tobacco Enforcement Section of the Wisconsin Department of Revenue.*

In the United States, 18-year-olds can legally drive, vote, and die for their country, but they cannot drink alcohol. Viewing this discrepancy in the law as a denial of their rights, today's teens are determined to beat the system. This results in a proliferation of false identification cards (IDs) and a nightly cat-and-mouse game between the youths and the law enforcement officers and alcohol beverage licensees who stand in their way.

Indeed, both law enforcement officers and retailers have become increasingly frustrated as false IDs have become a way of life for many thirsty 18-, 19-, and 20-year-olds. Aided by today's technology, these would-be patrons have become so sophisticated in their methods that they leave many alcohol beverage licensees and police officers shaking their heads.

Officials in Wisconsin faced similar concerns, which were compounded by the state's economic climate and environmental factors. In Wisconsin, a 40-ounce bottle of beer can cost less than a 33-ounce bottle of sparkling water, and the state beer tax has not increased since 1969. An abundance of bars and liquor stores provides teens with easy access to alcohol. Moreover, the Europeans who settled in the area over a century ago not only drink alcohol on a regular basis, they actually celebrate it through such festivals as Oktoberfest. Together, these factors make the state a prime target for underage drinkers using false IDs to purchase alcohol.

Many of these youths can be found on college campuses. One study concluded that as many as 22 percent of Wisconsin college students have false IDs,

Reprinted from "F.A.B. IDs: Fake, Altered, and Borrowed Cards," by Roger Johnson, *FBI Law Enforcement Bulletin*, February 1997.

although university police officers estimate numbers as high as 50 percent. One police detective at the University of Wisconsin at Madison has confiscated false IDs from every state in the nation, including Alaska and Hawaii.

Addressing the Problem

Tasked with enforcing alcohol beverage laws, special agents of the Alcohol and Tobacco Enforcement Section of the Wisconsin Department of Revenue knew that they would have to find a way to combat the state's underage drinking problem. They also realized that any strategy would need to have a broad impact for both law enforcement and the retail industry without draining the department's limited resources. With these requirements in mind, section agents developed a training program designed to help law enforcement officers and alcohol beverage retailers spot false IDs.

To begin, agents researched the methods used to manufacture forgeries by gathering information and false ID cards confiscated by university police departments, bar and liquor store owners located near college campuses, and in some cases, from the experts themselves, the counterfeiters. During the intelligence-gathering phase, it became clear that the cards generally fall into three categories: fake, altered, and borrowed.

Fake IDs

For the most part, fake, or counterfeit, IDs encompass two different types. Some closely resemble state driver's licenses. Others, such as identification cards manufactured by mail-order firms, may have no legal counterpart, making illegal ones harder to detect.

Still, both types of counterfeit cards may contain anomalies that can alert officials to their lack of authenticity. For example, a fake driver's license, when compared to the real thing, may be a different size, thickness, or color. Letters and numbers may differ in size, typeface, or placement, or they may be fuzzy. In fact, although many counterfeiters spend a great deal of time reproducing the front of the card, they may merely photocopy the reverse side, leaving blurred letters and/or dark images.

No matter how professional-looking it is, the front of the counterfeit card may miss the mark. The photograph may lack the quality of the motor vehicle card, producing a shadow or glare or giving the subject "red-eye." Finally, the state seal or logo may be missing or altered. Mail-order IDs may actually contain such phrases as "for personal use," "office use only," or "not a government document," a sure sign that the card is a fake.

Altered IDs

Altered IDs may exhibit signs of tampering in one or more places, including the numbers, the photograph, and the laminate. The birth date, driver's license number, height, and weight may be scratched or bleached out and inked over or cut out and reinserted. If altered, the numbers may be bumpy.

Changed numbers in the birth date may not correspond to the driver's license number, which many states code with the birth date and other identifying data. In Wisconsin, for example, the 7th and 8th numbers match the year of birth and the 9th through 11th numbers indicate the person's sex.

A photograph with bumpy surfaces or rough edges may have been inserted over the original. Because many states place their seal over the photograph, an ID altered in this manner would cover part of the seal.

Changes in the card's laminated cover often indicate tampering. It may contain glue lines or rough edges, especially near the photograph. Altered numbers may not match up after the laminate is put back into place. A shadowy or cloudy image on the card means that a new laminate covers the original.

Borrowed IDs

Oftentimes, minors borrow identification from individuals who can drink legally. Although appearances change, even subtle differences between the subject presenting the ID and the photograph and/or the physical description data on the card should be questioned.

Also included in this category are duplicate and expired cards. An expired driver's license or one marked "DUPL" may not belong to the person presenting it as identification.

"[False ID] cards generally fall into three categories: fake, altered, and borrowed."

After gathering a representative sample of fake, altered, and borrowed cards, agents photographed the cards and made them into slides, accentuating the points officers and retailers should examine in determining their validity. While most are examples of Wisconsin IDs, the slides also include those from other states. In addition to serving as a visual reference, these cards show that the same techniques used to alter and counterfeit cards in Wisconsin are used throughout the United States.

Conducting the Training

During the 4-hour training session, students [of the retailer and law enforcement training program] view the slide presentation, while listening to an informative lecture, which includes a review of the laws governing the manufacture and use of false IDs. Students also receive a close-up, hands-on look at the cards found in the slides.

Next, they put their newly acquired skills to the test. The instructor passes out 25 cards to the class; some, but not all, are altered or counterfeit. The students must determine which cards are bad and why. This practical exercise allows students to evaluate their ability to spot false IDs. As an added benefit, it gives law enforcement officers an appreciation for what liquor licensees confront on a daily basis.

An instructional text accompanies the visual aids. In addition to describing each card in detail, the text provides anecdotes to explain further how the cards were created, spotted, or seized.

Another handout given to the students is an ID-checking guide. The easy-to-use guide provides clues for identifying fake, altered, and borrowed cards. It also presents tips for obtaining corroborating information from cardholders.

A clever tactic involves casually conversing with the cardholder. For example, if an individual presents an ID card (as opposed to a driver's license) as proof of age, the retailer can inquire about the drive to the establishment. A person who admits to driving there should be able to present a license that matches the information on the ID card.

> *"Oftentimes, minors borrow identification from individuals who can drink legally."*

Officers and retailers also might question the carrier about some basic information on the card, such as the address, middle initial, or height and weight. Someone using a borrowed ID may not know the right answers. Another approach involves obtaining the person's signature, which may not match the one on the ID.

People carrying false IDs—whether fake, altered, or borrowed—rarely can produce backup documentation, whereas most people have several legitimate forms of identification. When confronted with a questionable ID, officers and retailers should ask for additional documentation, such as a Social Security card, a credit card, or a hunting or fishing license.

Working with the Beverage Industry

In classic examples of industry and government working together, the National Beer Wholesalers Association and the Beer Institute incorporated the ID-checking guide into their annual point-of-sale campaign aimed at thwarting underage drinking. Together, they have produced over 1 million laminated cards with tips for spotting false IDs. Printed in English, Spanish, and Korean, the cards go to retail establishments across the United States. The organizations also have teamed with independent breweries to produce a booklet that contains photographs of driver's licenses from the United States, Mexico, Canada, and the United Kingdom.

With assistance from revenue agents and funding from the National Highway Traffic Safety Administration, the Wisconsin Department of Transportation produced a training video, a laminated ID-checking guide, and a responsible-server packet, which gives alcohol servers and sellers a uniform policy to follow. Industry associations, including the Wisconsin Wholesale Beer Distributors Association, the Tavern League of Wisconsin, and the Wisconsin Tavern Hosts, cooperated in distributing these materials throughout the state.

Since the program's inception in 1988, Wisconsin revenue agents have provided free training to both industry officials and law enforcement officers in a number of forums. In addition to state and local officers and alcohol beverage retailers, recipients have included Pennsylvania Alcohol Beverage Control agents and members of the National Liquor Law Enforcement Association. Likewise, the class has been incorporated into Wisconsin's 400-hour police recruit training program, required for law enforcement certification in the state. This training is especially beneficial for new recruits, who often get assigned shifts where they encounter underage drinkers with false IDs.

Because Wisconsin law usually imposes civil penalties on youths who make or carry false IDs, no statewide statistics exist to gauge the full impact of this training program. Still, the class provides students with the ability to detect false IDs, a skill that officers can use in any situation where a subject presents identification. Moreover, the training has created a greater awareness in law enforcement, the beverage industry, and the community at large.

Like the rest of the 50 states, Wisconsin requires patrons to be 21 years old to buy and consume alcohol legally. At the same time, today's youths encounter tremendous peer and social pressure to drink. As the two forces clash, law enforcement faces a host of problems, most notably, a proliferation of false IDs.

At first glance, the problem of false ID use by underage drinkers in Wisconsin seemed insurmountable, especially in light of the state's economic climate and environmental factors. Yet, even with limited resources, agents from the Alcohol and Tobacco Enforcement Section of the Wisconsin Department of Revenue were able to develop and implement a broad strategy with statewide impact. With assistance from the private sector, they instituted a comprehensive training program designed to help law enforcement officers and beverage industry employees alike detect fake, altered, and borrowed IDs.

Bibliography

Books

Christine Bichler — *Teen Drinking*. New York: Rosen, 1999.

Morris E. Chafetz — *The Tyranny of Experts: Blowing the Whistle on the Cult of Expertise*. Lanham, MD: Madison, 1996.

Christina Chiu — *Teen Guide to Staying Sober*. New York: Rosen, 1998.

Janet Grosshandler — *Working Together Against Drunk Driving*. New York: Rosen, 1996.

David J. Hanson — *Alcohol Education: What We Must Do*. Westport, CT: Praeger, 1996.

David J. Hanson — *Preventing Alcohol Abuse*. Westport, CT: Praeger, 1995.

Jonathan Harris — *This Drinking Nation*. New York: Simon & Schuster, 1994.

Mark Gauvreau Judge — *Wasted: Tales of a Gen X Drunk*. Center City, MN: Hazelden Information Education, 1997.

Alagna Magdalena and Ruth Anne Ruiz — *Everything You Need to Know About the Dangers of Binge Drinking*. New York: Rosen, 2001.

Hank Nuwer — *Wrongs of Passage: Fraternities, Sororities, Hazing, and Binge Drinking*. Bloomington: Indiana University Press, 1999.

Robert M. O'Neil — *Alcohol Advertising on the Air: Beyond the Reach of Government?* Washington, DC: The Media Institute, 1997.

Edmund B. O'Reilly — *Sobering Tales: Narratives of Alcoholism and Recovery*. Amherst: University of Massachusetts Press, 1997.

Stanton Peele — *The Diseasing of America: How We Allowed Recovery Zealots to Convince We Are Out of Control*. San Francisco: Jossey-Bass, 1999.

Marc Alan Schuckit — *Educating Yourself About Alcohol and Other Drugs: A People's Primer*. New York: Plenum Press, 1998.

Elsie R. Shore et al. eds. — *Preventing Drunk Driving*. New York: Haworth Press, 1998.

Michael T. Windle — *Alcohol Use Among Adolescents*. Thousand Oaks, CA: Sage, 1999.

Periodicals

David Byrd	"Last Call for Alcohol?" *National Journal*, December 18, 1999.
Susan Cohen	"'Mom Doesn't Want to Know'; While Parents Are Paralyzed by Ambivalence Toward Alcohol, Teenagers Are Drinking Sooner and More Heavily," *Washington Post*, June 7, 1998.
CQ Researcher	"Alcohol Advertising," March 14, 1997. Available from 22nd St. NW, Washington, DC 20037.
CQ Researcher	"Drinking on Campus," March 20, 1998. Available from 22nd St. NW, Washington, DC 20037.
Amy Dickinson	"No School for Sots," *Time*, September 13, 1999.
Juliet Eilperin	"Beer Lobby Keeps Anti-Drug Drive Alcohol-Free," *Washington Post* July 23, 1999.
Linda A. Fletcher et al.	"Alcohol Home Delivery Services: A Source of Alcohol for Underage Drinkers," *Journal of Studies on Alcohol*, January 2000.
Marilyn Gardner	"When Teens Drink, Parents May Pay," *Christian Science Monitor*, September 6, 2000.
Neal Karlen	"Sobriety High," *Life*, February 1999.
Carolyn Kleiner	"Schools Turn off the Tap," *U.S. News & World Report*, August 30, 1999.
Laurie Leiber and Morris E. Chafetz,	"Should the Government Restrict Advertising of Alcoholic Beverages?" *Priorities*, vol. 9, no. 3, 1997. Available from www.acsh.org/publications/priorities/index.html.
David Leonhardt	"How Big Liquor Takes Aim at Teens," *Business Week*, May 19, 1997.
Jillian Lloyd	"Licensing Students to Drink?" *Christian Science Monitor*, May 28, 1996.
William W. London et al.	"The Effect of the Law on Underage Drinking and Driving," *American Journal of Public Health*, March 2000.
David L. Marcus	"Drinking to Get Drunk," *U.S. News & World Report*, March 27, 2000.
Don Oldenburg	"Kids and Alcohol: a Controversial Alternative to 'Just Say No,'" *Washington Post*, March 10, 1998.
Joyce Price	"New Battle About Evil Spirits," *Insight on the News*, February 1, 1999.
Maria Purdy	"Drinking Without Thinking," *Teen*, May 1998.
Naomi Schaefer	"Campus Crackdown," *National Review*, April 5, 1999.
Maureen Sirhal	"Fraternities on the Rocks," *Policy Review*, February/March 2000.

Bibliography

J.J. Thompson   "Plugging the Kegs," *U.S. News & World Report*, January 26, 1998.

Julie Weingarden   "The High Price of Popularity," *Teen*, June 1999.

Elizabeth M. Wheelan   "The Perils of Prohibition—Why We Should Lower the Drinking Age to 18," *Newsweek*, May 29, 1995.

Kate Zernike   "New Tactic on College Drinking: Play It Down," *New York Times*, October 3, 2000.

Organizations to Contact

The editors have compiled the following list of organizations concerned with the issues debated in this book. The descriptions are derived from materials provided by the organizations. All have publications or information available for interested readers. The list was compiled on the date of publication of the present volume; the information provided here may change. Be aware that many organizations take several weeks or longer to respond to inquiries, so allow as much time as possible.

Al-Anon Family Groups Headquarters
1600 Corporate Landing Parkway, Virginia Beach, VA 23454-5617
(757) 563-1600 • fax: (757) 563-1655
e-mail: WSO@alanon.org • website: www.al-anon.alateen.org

Al-Anon is a fellowship of men, women, and children whose lives have been affected by an alcoholic family member or friend. Alateen consists primarily of teenaged Al-Anon members who hold meetings in order to share experiences and learn how to deal with the effects of another person's drinking. Al-Anon/Alateen publications include several books, the monthly magazine *The Forum*, the semiannual *Al-Anon Speaks Out*, the bimonthly *Alateen Talk*, and pamphlets, such as *To the Mother and Father of an Alcoholic*, *Dear Mom & Dad*, and *Alcoholism, the Family Disease*.

Alcoholics Anonymous (AA)
Grand Central Station, PO Box 459, New York, NY 10163
(212) 870-3400 • fax: (212) 870-3003
website: www.aa.org

Alcoholics Anonymous is a worldwide fellowship of sober alcoholics, whose recovery is based on Twelve Steps. AA requires no dues or fees and accepts no outside funds. It is self-supporting through voluntary contributions of members. It is not affiliated with any other organization. AA's primary purpose is to carry the AA message to the alcoholic who still suffers. Its publications include the pamphlets *A Brief Guide to Alcoholics Anonymous*, *Young People and AA*, and *A Message to Teenagers . . . How to Tell When Drinking Is Becoming a Problem*.

American Beverage Institute (ABI)
1775 Pennsylvania Ave. NW, Suite 1200, Washington, DC 20006
(202) 463-7110 • fax: (202) 463-7107
e-mail: abi@abionline.org • website: www.abionline.org

The American Beverage Institute is a coalition of restaurants and on-premise retailers committed to the responsible serving of alcoholic beverages. The ABI is involved in research, consumer education, and legislative outreach. It publishes the monthly *ABI Newsletter*, legislative alerts, and the report ".08% Debate: What's the Harm?"

The Beer Institute
122 C St. NW, Suite 750, Washington, DC 20001-2150
(202) 737-2337
e-mail: info@beerinstitute.org • website: www.beerinst.org

The Beer Institute is the official trade association for the American brewing industry. It promotes drinking in moderation and has implemented programs such as alcohol awareness curricula in schools and public service announcements to combat underage drinking and drunk driving. *Focus on Underage Drinking* and *Guarding Against Drug and Alcohol Abuse in the Nineties* are among its many publications.

Canadian Centre on Substance Abuse (CCSA)

75 Albert St., Suite 300, Ottawa ON K1P 5E7 Canada
(613) 235-4048 ext. 222 • fax: (613) 235-8108
e-mail: info@ccsa.ca • website: www.ccsa.ca

The CCSA is a Canadian clearinghouse on substance abuse. It works to disseminate information on the nature, extent, and consequences of substance abuse and to support and assist organizations involved in substance abuse treatment, prevention, and educational programming. The CCSA publishes reports, policy documents, brochures, research papers, the newsletter *Action News,* and several books, including *Canadian Profile: Alcohol, Tobacco, and Other Drugs.* Its website provides resources and information on youth drinking.

Center for Science in the Public Interest (CSPI)—Alcohol Policies Project

1875 Connecticut Ave. NW, Suite 300, Washington, DC 20009
(202) 332-9110 • fax: (202) 265-4954
e-mail: cspi@cspinet.org • website: www.cspinet.org/booze

CSPI launched the Alcohol Policies Project to reduce the devastating health and social consequences of drinking. The project's prevention-oriented policy strategy is aimed at curbing alcohol-related problems by advocating advertising reforms, increased excise taxes, and expanded warning requirements. Its publications include the quarterly newsletter *BoozeNews,* fact sheets on topics such as binge drinking and alcohol advertising, and the report *Last Call for High-Risk Bar Promotions That Target College Students.*

Distilled Spirits Council of the United States (DISCUS)

1250 Eye St. NW, Suite 400, Washington, DC 20005
(202) 628-3544 • fax: (202) 682-8888
website: www.discus.org

The Distilled Spirits Council of the United States is the national trade association representing producers and marketers of distilled spirits sold in the United States. It seeks to ensure the responsible advertising and marketing of distilled spirits to adult consumers and to prevent such advertising and marketing from targeting individuals below the legal purchase age. DISCUS fact sheets and pamphlets, including *Social Responsibility and Public Education,* are available at its website.

Mothers Against Drunk Driving (MADD)

511 E. John Carpenter Frwy., #700, Irving, TX 75062
(800) 438-6233
e-mail: info@madd.org • website: www.madd.org

Mothers Against Drunk Driving seeks to act as the voice of victims of drunk driving accidents by speaking on their behalf to communities, businesses, and educational groups and by providing materials for use in medical facilities and health and driver education programs. Its website's "Under 21" section provides information for teens about alcohol and drunk driving. MADD publishes brochures, the newsletter *MADD in Action,* and *Driven* magazine.

National Association for Children of Alcoholics (NACoA)
11426 Rockville Pike, Suite 100, Rockville, MD 20852
(888) 554-COAS (554-2627) • fax: (301) 468-0987
e-mail: nacoa@erols.com • website: www.health.org/nacoa

NACoA is the only national nonprofit membership organization working on behalf of children of alcoholics. Its mission is to advocate for all children and families affected by alcoholism and other drug dependencies. The association publishes books, pamphlets, videos, educational kits, and the bimonthly *NACoA Network Newsletter.*

National Center on Addiction and Substance Abuse (CASA)
Columbia University, 152 West 57th St., New York, NY 10019
(212) 841-5200 • fax: (212) 956-8020
website: www.casacolumbia.org

The National Center on Addiction and Substance Abuse brings together all professional disciplines needed to study and combat substance abuse, including alcohol abuse. CASA assesses what works in prevention, treatment, and law enforcement; informs Americans about the economic and social costs of substance abuse; and removes the stigma of substance abuse. Publications include the reports *Substance Abuse and the American Adolescent: A Report by the Commission on Substance Abuse Among America's Adolescents* and *Dangerous Liaisons: Substance Abuse and Sex.*

The National Clearinghouse for Alcohol and Drug Information (NCADI)
P.O. Box 2345, Rockville, MD 20847-2345
(800) 729-6686 • fax: (301) 468-6433
e-mail: info@health.org • website: www.health.org

The NCADI is the information service of the Center for Substance Abuse Prevention of the Substance Abuse and Mental Health Services Administration in the U.S. Department of Health & Human Services. NCADI is the world's largest resource for current information and materials concerning substance abuse. The organization distributes fact sheets, brochures, pamphlets, monographs, posters, and video tapes and provides prevention, intervention, and treatment resources to families, schools, and professionals. Its publications include *Patterns of Alcohol Use Among Adolescents and Associations with Emotional and Behavioral Problems, Alarming Costs of Youth Alcohol Abuse*, and *Tips for Teens About Alcohol.*

National Council on Alcoholism and Drug Dependence (NCADD)
12 West 21st St., New York, NY 10010
(212) 206-6770 • fax: (212) 645-1690
e-mail: national@ncadd.org • website: www.ncadd.org

NCADD is a volunteer health organization that helps individuals overcome addictions, develops substance abuse prevention and education programs for youth, and advises the federal government on drug and alcohol policies. It operates the Campaign to Prevent Kids From Drinking. Publications include fact sheets such as "Youth, Alcohol and Other Drugs," brochures, the quarterly newsletter *NCADD Amethyst*, and the monthly newsletter *NCADD Washington Report.*

National Institute on Alcohol Abuse and Alcoholism (NIAAA)
Willco Building, 6000 Executive Blvd., Bethesda, MD 20892-7003
(301) 496-4000
e-mail: niaaaweb-r@exchange.nih.gov • website: www.niaaa.nih.gov

NIAAA supports and conducts biomedical and behavioral research on the causes, consequences, treatment, and prevention of alcoholism and alcohol-related problems. Its College Drinking Initiative seeks to provide the NIAAA, policymakers, and college presidents with research on campus prevention and treatment programs. The NIAAA publishes the quarterly journal *Alcohol Research & Health* (formerly *Alcohol Health & Research World*), *Alcohol Alert* bulletins, pamphlets, and reports.

Students Against Destructive Decisions! (SADD)

SADD National, Box 800, Marlboro, MA 01752
(800) 787-5777 • fax: (508) 481-5759
website: www.saddonline.com

Also known as Students Against Driving Drunk, SADD's mission is to prevent under-age drinking and drug use and to focus attention on the consequences of other decisions such as smoking, violence, and sexually transmitted diseases. SADD promotes a no-use message of alcohol and other drugs and encourages students not to participate in activi-ties with destructive consequences. It publishes a newsletter, press releases, and also provides a "Contract for Life" that can be used to increase parent-child communication about alcohol and drug-related decisions.

The Wine Institute

425 Market St., Suite 1000, San Francisco, CA 94105
(415) 512-0151 • fax: (415) 442-0742
e-mail: communications@wineinstitute.org • website: www.wineinstitute.org

The Wine Institute introduces and advocates public policy measures to enhance the en-vironment for the responsible consumption and enjoyment of wine. It publishes the monthly newsletter *Newsflash* and the reports "American Health Association Advisory Acknowledges 'Potentially Sizable Health Benefit' of Alcohol" and "Study Finds Bet-ter Brain Functioning Among Moderate Alcohol Consuming Women."

Internet Resources

Alcohol: Problems and Solutions Website

website: www2.potsdam.edu/alcohol-info

This website describes alcohol use and abuse along with effective ways to reduce or elim-inate drinking problems such as underage drinking, drinking and driving, and binge drink-ing. The *In Their Own Words* section contains interviews with experts on a wide variety of alcohol-related issues, *In the News* provides current news articles for downloading, and *In My Opinion* offers essays including "It's Better to Teach Safe Use of Alcohol."

Drink Smart

website: www.drinksmart.org

Drink Smart is an electronic magazine, based in Canada, that believes encouraging re-sponsible drinking by young people who have reached the legal age is a laudable goal. Drink Smart publishes personal stories on drinking and driving, the effects of alcohol and families, and attitudes toward drinking among teens and at colleges.

The Stanton Peele Addiction Website

website: www.peele.net

Stanton Peele has been researching and writing about addiction for thirty years. His con-troversial approach negates the American medical model of addiction as a disease. In-stead, he views it as a behavior which can be overcome through maturity, improved cop-ing skills, and better self-management and self-esteem. His website includes an "Ask Stanton" question and answer section and an extensive virtual library of articles available for viewing. Peele has also authored several books, including *The Truth About Addiction and Recovery* and *The Diseasing of America*, which may be ordered from the website.

Index